The First Ever

ENGLISH

OLIMPICK GAMES

The First Ever

ENGLISH
OLIMPICK GAMES

CELIA HADDON

Hodder & Stoughton
LONDON SYDNEY AUCKLAND

British Library Cataloguing in Publication Data
A record for this book is available from the British Library

ISBN 0 340 86283 1

Printed and bound in Great Britain by Clays Ltd, St Ives plc

The paper and board used in this paperback are natural recyclable products
made from wood grown in sustainable forests. The manufacturing proc-
esses conform to the country of origin.

Hodder & Stoughton
A Division of Hodder Headline Ltd
338 Euston Road
London NW1 3BH
www.madaboutbooks.com

Contents

Thanks

I would like to thank the following for their help during the writing of this book. Dr Francis Burns, secretary of the Robert Dover's Games Society, was generous in his aid. His new book *Robert Dover's Cotswold Olimpick Games: Annalia Dubrensia (1636) and Other Poems* (ISBN 0-9507487-3-0) is must reading for those who wish to pursue the subject. Terry Brown of the Company of Maisters helped me understand the nature of English martial arts. He is dedicated to their revival and his book *English Martial Arts* gives a complete overview on the subject. Terry Brown gives tuition, puts on displays and can be contacted via the Company of Maisters website: www.maisters.demon.co.uk. These martial arts need real courage and endurance, and are for real men (of either sex!). Matthew Alexander of the Guildford Museum explained the nature and mechanism of Dover's Castle to me. Denise Lafrance of the Public Library in Dover, New Hampshire, alerted me to the fact that her town took its name from Robert Dover. John Goulstone helped me with information about ancient English games and festivals. Don Anthony, the Olympics heritage expert, gave me help and encouragement. On mazes I had help from Jo Edkins and Lindsay Heyes. There were many others who gave help and support including Dorothy Hart of the Tourist Information Office in Chipping Campden and the editor of the *Olympic Review* magazine of the International Olympic Association in Switzerland. Last of all, I should like to thank Jilly Wilkinson, whose pictures of the modern Olimpicks adorn the last chapter.

Acknowledgements

The author wishes to thank the following for permission to reproduce the pictures listed:

The British Library

By permission of The British Library: pictures from *Annalia Dubrensia*, ed E. R.Vyvyan (*shelfmark 11630.33.5*), on pages 1, 3, 5 ,7, 9, 10, 13, 17, 33, 42, 48, 52, 63 (half page), 67, 68, 69, 72, 75, 78, 79, 89, 93, 101, 121, 149, 166, 175 and 189.

By permission of The British Library: pictures from *Poly-Olbion* by Michael Drayton (*shelfmark 11612.i.7*), which appear on pages 20, 23, 26, 38, 57, 58, 60 and 80.

Jilly Wilkinson

Additional pictures have been drawn for this book by Jilly Wilkinson, who can be contacted via the author.

I would also like to thank Penny Mills for her splendid book design and Judith Longman for her intelligence and sense of fun.

The First Ever
ENGLISH
OLIMPICK GAMES

AN EXTRACT FROM
THE ORIGINAL INTRODUCTION
TO THE 1636 BOOK, ADDRESSED TO
Robert Dover

Since those Quinquenalia or Olympic Games
– celebrated every fifth year only – begun by
Hercules, and for many succeeding ages
continued by all semones, heroes, and prime
princes of Greece, are now utterly abandoned, and
their memories almost extinguished; since you to
whom I may not unproperly give the denomina-
tion of an hero of this our age, have in these your
famous Annalia, or yearly Celebrations, not only
revived the memory of the former, but adorned
these your Cotswold Hills with such ovations and
triumphs as may continue their memory to all
posterity; first craving your pardon, I commend
myself to you for the present, and your name ... to
perpetuity.

MATTHEW WALBANCKE

INTRODUCTION

The first ever Olimpicks are an astonishing episode in English history. I came across a glancing reference to them in an eighteenth-century history of Gloucestershire and was amazed to discover that the modern Olympic Games movement started four centuries ago.

As I write, London is putting in a bid for the Olympic Games, and the proposed year – 2012 – when we hope to run the Olympic Games will also be the four hundredth anniversary of the first time England held games of this kind.

The original Olimpicks have left only a small trace in written history. Most of what we know about them comes from the celebratory anthology of poetry *Annalia Dubrensia*, published in 1636. The contemporary accounts of the Games are in verse, not prose. Their founder, Robert Dover, wrote one of the poems and these sixty-eight lines of poetry are his only account.

Victorian antiquarians republished this poetry anthology with the hopeful suggestion that William Shakespeare visited the Games. Maybe he did. We do not know. Then in the 1960s the poems were again published, this time with a history of Robert Dover and his Games by Christopher Whitfield.

The present secretary of the Robert Dover's Games Society, Dr Francis Burns, had started researching them in the 1960s and could be said to be the Games' official historian. His devotion not only to the Games' history and their origins, but also to their continuation, has a thoroughness and commitment I cannot equal.

I have used just a few extracts from the original poetry collection. Readers who would like to read all the poems can find them in Dr Francis Burns' latest book, *Robert Dover's Cotswold Olimpick Games: Annalia Dubrensia (1636) and Other Poems* (ISBN 0-9507487-3-0). This and his booklet, *Heigh for Cotswold! Robert Dover's Olimpick Games,* are available from the Robert Dover's Games Society on www. olimpickgames.co.uk.

But the best memorial of the first ever English Olympics is to be found every Whitsun Friday evening on Dover's Hill, a Cotswold escarpment high above the Vale of Evesham. Go and see a little piece of Olympic heritage and history in action. You will enjoy it.

Celia Haddon

Summer 2004

TO MY NOBLE FRIEND
Mr Robert Dover
ON HIS ANNUAL ASSEMBLIES
UPON COTSWOLD

The country wakes and whirlings have appeared
Of late like foreign pastimes. Carnivals,
Palm and rush bearing, harmless Whitsun ales,
Running at quintain, May games, general plays,
By some more nice than wise, of latter days,
Have in their standings, lectures, exercises
Been so reproved, traduced, condemned for vices
Profane and heathenish, that now few dare
Set them afoot. The Hocktide pastimes are
Declined, if not deserted, so that now
All public merriments, I know not how,
Are questioned for their lawfulness; whereby
Society grew sick, was like to die.
And had not jovial Dover well invented
A means whereby to have the same prevented,
Love feasts and friendly intercourse had perished,
Which now are kept alive by him, and cherished ...

JOHN TRUSSELL

[16]

Chapter 1

THE FIRST EVER
OLIMPICKS –
Sponsorship and Support

Cannons roared out over the grassy Cotswold hillside. Athletes and other contestants took their places. A well-dressed man, wearing a hat with a feather in it and riding a white horse, sounded a bugle. The glory that was Greece's Olympic Games had come to England's green and pleasant land.

The year was 1612. The Stuart King James I was on the throne. The onlookers and the athletes were wearing doublet and hose and the women were in long skirts. The first ever English Olimpicks was under way. Local shepherds sang, danced and took part in sports contests while landowners, clergymen, poets and even the occasional visiting courtier looked on under the benevolent eye of Robert Dover, a local lawyer. It was the emergence of what was, nearly three centuries later, to be the modern Olympic movement. England's Olympic heritage started on that Cotswold hillside.

The long peaceful rule of Queen Elizabeth I had come to an end, and the succession of her cousin James I had, despite fears, been without conflict. The new king had secured the future of the Church of England, keeping England Protestant rather than Catholic. 'There had been a long serene calm of peace and men minded nothing but peace and luxury,' wrote the antiquarian John Aubrey, looking back wistfully at the first forty years of the seventeenth century.

We don't know exactly which year the first English Olimpicks started, but we do know that they were supported by no less a personage than James I. And after they had become an annual fixture their existence was celebrated with a book of poetry, *Annalia Dubrensia*, which is the main source of detail about what went on.

This book was published in 1636 when the Olimpicks had been established for many years. Various later documents have suggested differing dates from 1601 to 1612 for their first appearance. But a nineteenth-century poster, which draws upon local knowledge, suggests 1612, the year after Robert Dover had settled in the Cotswolds, where he was to practise as a lawyer.

Nor do we know whether the first ever English Olimpicks started from nothing or whether they took over from an existing local celebration. The location was a hillside above the small Cotswold village of Weston sub Edge, near the parish boundary of the nearby market town of Chipping Campden. Not far off is an ancient standing stone, the Kiftsgate Stone, which marks the moot (or meeting) place of the old Saxon hundred and may even date further back into prehistory.

In those days the area, about 500 acres, was not split up into separate fields and enclosed with boundary hedges or fences as it is now. Meadow grassland of the kind that covered the

hillside was held in common, with individuals from nearby villages having the right to graze a certain number of animals every year at set times. Land suitable for ploughing, in the areas less steep than the hillside grassland, was strip-farmed in open fields with only banked-up earth or turf separating one man's ploughland strip from another.

Kingcombe Plain, as it was then called, was and is a natural amphitheatre. Those sitting on the side of the hill could look down on the performers below and out over the plain below. Nowadays Dover's Hill, as the Kingcombe Plain is known, seems in the back of beyond, but then it had – by seventeenth-century standards – good communications. In the valley below ran what was then an important road to London, with the poor walking and the gentry riding horse-back or in horse-drawn vehicles. Dover showed a good eye for the ground in choosing this particular hillside.

His choice may have been influenced by the fact that Kingcombe Plain was already the site for a much smaller local Whitsun event. If so, Dover took it over and re-organised it. But it is clear from the reaction of those who mentioned the Games that, whatever their origins, these Olimpicks were something different, something which seemed quite remarkable to his contemporaries. There were traditional fairs, festivals, wakes and church ales held in the British countryside, and then there were Robert Dover's Olimpick Games.

As the Games continued year after year, they gathered importance as a symbol of Merry England – a nostalgic phrase first in print as early as 1552. Part of their significance to their supporters came from the feeling that this way of life was vanishing. The old queen, Queen Elizabeth, had died and there was a feeling of nostalgia for the past century. People looked back and remembered the old traditions – the church festivals, the fairs, the countryside revels as they once had been. The past began to take on the lustre of a golden age.

In truth, Tudor England had been a worrying time of changes for ordinary people. The disruptions started when the monasteries of Catholic England were looted and destroyed by Henry VIII. Then Henry's son, the boy king Edward VI, had brought in a new prayer book in English and done away with most of the religious processions and holy days. His successor and half-sister Queen Mary had restored the Catholic faith, burned Protestants and tried to restore the old church traditions, failing only to wrest the church lands from their new lay possessors!

Then back came a Protestant, Elizabeth I. She had aimed at a middle-of-the-road Protestantism and had done so without too much shedding of blood. True, the Catholic priests who surreptitiously entered England to minister to the faithful were often imprisoned, tortured and executed. But lay Catholics who otherwise kept out of trouble were merely fined for not going to church, and those who outwardly followed the Church of England by turning up on Sundays were usually left alone by the authorities.

By tradition the games of Merry England had been linked to the church year. The ritual year started with Epiphany, proceeded through Lent and Easter to Whitsun, Lammas and Martinmas, then back through Advent to Christmas. Saints' days or holy days marked the change of the seasons with fasts or feasts.

Working people did not have yearly vacations or even Saturdays off. They worked six days a week with only one day, Sunday, as a day of rest without work. The only other holidays from work were literally holy days that were celebrated by the Church. Before the Protestant reformers got to work, the Church had been the focal point not just of the Sunday and holy day services but also of the games and celebrations afterwards. These were often held in the churchyard itself.

Some folklore enthusiasts have argued that these celebrations go right back to pre-Christian times and that, just as the Christian Church took over the places and buildings of pre-Christian worship, so it took over the ritual celebrations too. It is an argument that would have been familiar to some of the disapproving Puritans of the seventeenth century. Whitsun, the time when the disciples of Christ were visited by the Holy Ghost, was an important holy day, often marked by a parish Whitsun ale or a wake.

A church ale was the equivalent of today's money-raising church fêtes – with ale instead of tea. Money or provisions were collected in advance, and ale was brewed ready for the day on which it would be sold. Profits went to the church or to the local poor. The sum raised could be substantial. 'There were no rates for the poor in my grandfather's days; but for Kingston St Michael (no small parish) the church-ale of Whitsuntide did the business,' wrote John Aubrey in the second half of the seventeenth century.

As well as the sale of ale, there was feasting. 'Tarts and custards, creams and cakes are the junkets still at wakes,' wrote the seventeenth-century poet and clergyman Robert Herrick. There were rustic music, games and sports. There were morris dancers and perhaps plays put on by the locals or by travelling players. Sometimes a Whitsun Lord and Lady, or maybe a Robin Hood and Maid Marion, were chosen as figureheads for the celebrations.

Looking back to the time of his grandfather and full of

nostalgia for this lost Merry England of a generation earlier, John Aubrey recalled: 'The young people were there too, and had dancing, bowling, shooting at butts, etc., the ancients sitting gravely by, and looking on. All things were civil and without scandal.' This was the golden glow of hindsight.

Critics of church ales, and they were not all Puritans, complained of drunken behaviour and sexual licence at these local celebrations. Even Robert Herrick, a poet in favour of country celebrations, admits that at the end of the day's festivities any arguments were 'drenched in ale, or drowned in beer'.

Protestant reformers particularly disliked the combination of religious tradition and folk practice such as the election of a Robin Hood – in their eyes a blasphemous mixture of popery and paganism. During the reign of the boy king Edward VI, Bishop Hugh Latimer had been visiting a parish in a nearby diocese on May Day, also the saints' day of St Philip and St James. He found the church shut. The whole parish had gone into the fields and woods to celebrate May Day and 'gather for Robin Hood'. Latimer was shocked. 'It is no laughing matter, my friends, it is a weeping matter, a heavy matter, a heavy matter, under the pretence for gathering for Robin Hood, a traitor and a thief, to put out a preacher, to have his office less esteemed, to prefer Robin Hood before the ministration of God's word.'

Despite the opposition of Protestant reformers like Latimer and local magistrates worried about civil disorder, many of the May games and Whitsun ales had nevertheless survived in country parishes. It may have been one of these Whitsun ales that Dover took over and transformed into his Olimpick Games. His Games were carefully designed to avoid some of the controversies surrounding church ales, and were attended not just by the local shepherds but also by the surrounding gentry.

He may even have asked for advance permission from King James before starting up his festival. Writing half a century or so later, the antiquarian Anthony à Wood of Oxford, not always accurate on the subject of the Cotswold Olimpicks, claimed that Dover got 'leave from King James' to start the Games. Even if he did not ask for advance permission, Dover would have had a good idea of what kind of sporting activities had the approval of the king.

For in 1598, James VI of Scotland, later also to become James I of England, had published *Basilicon Doron*, a book of advice to his son and heir, Henry, then aged only four. Advice or etiquette books for princes were a recognised literary genre at the time. *Basilicon Doron* was a great success, being translated first from the Middle Scots in which James had written it to English the following year and then on into several other languages. A revised edition came out in 1603, the year of his accession to the English throne and nine years before the first Olimpicks.

It was in this book that the king had made clear his approval of country games. In order to promote good feeling among the common people towards their king, James wrote

certain days in the year would be appointed, for delighting the people with public spectacles of all honest games, and exercise of arms: as also for convening of neighbours, or entertaining friendship and heartliness, by honest feasting and merriness: For I cannot see what greater superstition can be in making plays and lawful games in May, and good cheer at Christmas, than in eating fish in Lent, and upon Fridays, the papists as well using the one as the other: so that always the Sabbaths be kept holy, and no unlawful pastime be used.

Not surprisingly, therefore, King James gave his approval, whether in advance or after the Games had started, to the Cotswold Olimpicks. He may even, as a sign of royal favour, have given a coat of arms, with the motto 'Do Ever Good', a word play on the lawyer's surname, to Robert Dover. Dover's grandson claimed this had occurred, though the heraldic authorities in 1682 refused to accept his claim.

Royal sponsorship came in another indisputable and visible form – second-hand clothes, passed on by Endymion Porter, from the nearby village of Aston sub Edge. 'Endymion Porter Esq., a native of that county, and a servant to that king ... did, to encourage Dover, give him some of the king's old clothes, with a hat and feather and ruff, purposely to grace him and consequently the solemnity,' Anthony à Wood tells us.

King James could certainly have afforded to send a few cast-offs via the courtier Endymion Porter. He had plenty to spare. In one five-year period he bought sixty new cloaks, more than eight waistcoats, a new suit every ten days, a new pair of stockings, boots and garters every four or five days and a new pair of gloves every day.

And, of course, clothes were worth more in those days. People did not throw away their old clothes; they passed them on – to relatives, to their servants or to the poor. Clothes were mended and patched and often went through several owners before being used as rags. They were so valuable that they featured in many wills.

Typical was the will of 1675, of a farmer from the same

village as Robert Dover though dying well after Dover's time. William Russell of Childswickham left his best cloth coat to a friend, and the breeches and waistcoat of the same cloth to 'my kinsman'. His second cloth suit, the less valuable one, went to a young man and the will added: 'I give an old pair of breeches to Will Baker.' Even an old pair of breeches was a worthwhile legacy.

Today the idea of supporting a sporting occasion by giving various second-hand garments seems comic, but clothes were much more than fashion items in that century and more even than valuable possessions. They had a powerful symbolic meaning. Most servants of great men wore livery – clothes that were a badge of office. Indeed, many servants were paid not just in cash but also in perks and gifts, which usually included clothing.

The rich dressed differently from the poor. Puritans dressed differently from Cavaliers. What you wore defined who you were – your occupation, your religious beliefs and your social status. If you dressed above your status you attracted considerable criticism, and if below, mockery.

Some of this symbolic significance still clings to modern

clothing. The unwanted clothes of pop stars like Elton John raise money for charity. After her death, the dresses of the late Diana Princess of Wales were also auctioned for charity, and if the tabloids are to be believed, today's royal family still give their cast-offs to their servants.

So when Robert Dover opened his Olimpicks dressed in clothes that had been worn by the king, it was a powerful message. He was wearing the badge of royalty. The first ever Olimpick Games were sponsored by the highest in the land, the monarch himself.

A CONGRATULATORY POEM
TO MY POETICAL AND
Learned Noble Friends …

I cannot tell what planet ruled, when I
First undertook this mirth, this jollity,
Nor can I give account to you at all,
How this conceit into my brain did fall,
Or how I durst assemble, call together,
Such multitudes of people as come hither.
    Whilst Greece frequented active sports and plays
From other men they bore away the praise;
Their commonwealths did flourish, and their men
Unmatchèd were for worth and honour then;
But when they once those pastimes did forsake,
And unto drinking did themselves betake,
So base they grew, that at this present day
They are not men, but moving lumps of clay …

Let those that be of melancholy form,
And pensive spirits, fret themselves, and storm;
Let snarling Envy bark, pine, and grow mad;
Let carping Momus pouting be, and sad;
And let Content and Mirth all those attend,
That do all harmless honest sports defend!

ROBERT DOVER

[32]

Chapter 2

ROBERT DOVER
− FOUNDER OF THE
First Olimpicks

S o who was this country lawyer who became famous to his contemporaries for starting the Olimpick Games yet who seems to have had no great agenda in starting them? For him they were just 'this mirth, this jollity'. Although this Cotswold lawyer argues in his poem that sports kept young men away from drinking and smoking, he speaks of them as recreational rather than competitive.

Robert Dover seems to have been a man who, above all, enjoyed pastimes and good company. He was, in the eyes of his friends, the paradigm of a good lawyer, a rarity in the human jungle of the seventeenth century and indeed today. Lawyers, then as now, were not generally loved.

He was praised for being both honest and helpful. In a poem written about his Olimpicks, one of his friends, a clergyman named Nicholas Wallington, wrote:

> Thou … may'st a mirror of all lawyers be,
> In thy profession or thy honesty!
> It is a wonder that I ne'er could see
> That creature yet that ere spake ill of thee!
> The best are glad to gain thy company
> And do resort thy house most frequently.

Other friends described him as worthy, jovial, witty, generous and noble, and a picture emerges of a man who is honest, good company, hospitable and fun-loving.

It is in the early life and education of this man that we may perhaps see the origins of the Olimpick nature of his Games. For perhaps the most significant thing about Robert Dover was that he came from a Catholic family and was given at least as much of a Catholic education as was possible.

Born in Norfolk in 1582, during the reign of Protestant Queen Elizabeth, Robert Dover became a student of Queen's College, Cambridge, where he matriculated at the age of thirteen. This early age may be significant, for had he matriculated a year later he would have had to take an oath acknowledging the queen's authority over the Church and renouncing the authority of the pope. This oath was the passport to many of the official jobs in England.

Some four years after matriculation, young Dover's name appears in the records of Wisbech Castle, described as the servant of a Catholic priest though clearly he is not of the servant class. The clue lies in Wisbech Castle itself, which was where the authorities confined priests and lay Catholics who were not going to be executed but needed to be put out of the way. Sending a son there as a servant was a way of ensuring that the boy got a Catholic education.

The authorities cracked down on this practice and sent home the boys at Wisbech, including the

seventeen-year-old Robert Dover, but they noted in their official report that his parents did attend their parish church. So the Dover family would have been what were known as 'church papists', at heart Catholics but willing to conform to the law and attend the parish church.

By doing so, they could avoid a heavy fine of twelve pence that was levied on each occasion of absence – a fine large enough to be a serious deterrent to all but the really rich. So becoming a church papist was their way out of a dilemma. It was an uncomfortable situation for believers, because the

Catholic authorities in Rome declared it unlawful to attend heretical Protestant services.

Many Catholics, while attending morning or evening services, therefore tried hard to avoid taking Protestant communion. 'A church papist,' wrote the essayist John Earle in 1628,

> is one that parts his religion betwixt his conscience and his purse, and comes to church not to serve God but the king. The face of the law makes him wear the mask of the gospel which he uses not as a means to save his soul but [to save his] charges. He loves popery well, but is loath to lose by it … He kneels with the congregation, but prays by himself, and asks God forgiveness for coming thither.

From his parents, Robert Dover learned both the Catholic faith and also the wisdom of obeying the civil authorities. The Dover family was neither rich enough to live off their estates nor aristocratic enough to have their own coat of arms (though, as we have seen, Robert Dover's grandsons tried to claim that King James gave him one). Their son had

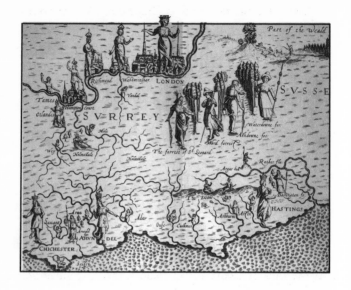

to have a profession in order to earn a living; as a Catholic Robert Dover could not go into the Church, so becoming a lawyer was the obvious alternative.

When he next turns up in the educational records, it is as a law student at Gray's Inn. The choice of Inn may be significant: during the reign of Elizabeth Gray's Inn had been particularly slow in enforcing religious conformity, and in 1585 not only had various Catholic priests sheltered there but masses had even been said on the premises.

One of the oddities of life in Gray's Inn, and in the other Inns of Court, was that while some Catholic lawyers were expelled or even imprisoned for their faith, other known Catholics could practise law without disturbance. This relative tolerance may have been another reason why Robert Dover, and his elder brother Richard before him, had chosen an education there.

The Inns of Court were the educational equivalent of Oxford and Cambridge, attended not only by would-be lawyers but also by students who had no intention of prac-tising the law. The latter were noblemen and 'gallant young gentlemen', being educated for life rather than the bar. At the Inns of Court a man could study the humanities, Greek and Latin, and history. Nowadays, when a classical education in Latin and Greek has all but disappeared, we forget that any educated man of the time would have been schooled from the tender age of six or seven in Latin texts. Education *was* Latin, and higher education was increasingly including Greek as well. By the accession of Queen Elizabeth most grammar schools expected to teach Greek.

Robert Dover, as a lawyer, would have needed to read Latin with the ease that we read English. He may also have had some Greek. Gray's Inn became the most prestigious, and most scholastic, of the Inns of Court during the reign of Elizabeth. The more enthusiastic among the Gray's Inn students would have read the Greek poet Pindar in the original, and been familiar with his odes on the Olympic and other ancient games. Even if Dover did not read Greek he would have known of these.

Sir Philip Sidney, for instance, certainly knew the odes and noted that some people couldn't see why Pindar made so much of these ancient games. 'A man may say that Pindar many times praiseth highly victories of small moment, matters rather of sport than virtue … so indeed the chief fault was in the time and custom of the Greeks, who set those toys at so high a price, that Philip of Macedon reckoned a horse-race won at Olympus among his three fearful felicities,' he wrote disapprovingly.

Gray's Inn relaxations were notable, too, being feasts, revels, masques and plays. Over several days during Christmastime in 1594, for instance, before Dover was admitted to the Inn, there is a record of the 'daily revels and such like sports, which were usual' as well as 'diverse grand nights for the entertainment of strangers'. Shakespeare's *Comedy of Errors* was put on there, probably for its first performance, as well as 'dancing and revelling with gentlewomen'.

It is at Gray's Inn that Robert Dover may have developed his taste for sports and revels. He became known as a man of wit, and at some point in his career wrote a pastoral poem, a popular genre of the day, and a poem or pageant titled 'The Wandering Jew'. The texts of both, if they were ever published, are now lost, but Peter Heylin, a London clergyman, wrote a congratulatory poem about them, hailing Dover as a better poet than Edmund Spenser, well-known author of the Elizabethan epic poem *The Faerie Queen*.

It was at Gray's Inn, either as a student or later in his career, that Dover met Matthew Walbancke, the bookseller and publisher, who had a book business within the passage of the Gray's Inn gateway. Walbancke was to play his part in the Dover Olimpicks by publishing the book of poems, *Annalia Dubrensia*, which celebrated the Games.

By the seventeenth century, some of the Dover family had probably become more conformist. Dover's sister Anne had married a Church of England vicar and in 1602 had moved with him to the Gloucestershire village of

Saintbury, where he became rector. Her brother Richard had also moved into the nearby town of Evesham. Nine years after his sister's move into Saintbury, Robert Dover joined her in the village, buying the lease of a house there.

It was a time when the work available for lawyers was growing in Gloucestershire and their numbers were increasing to meet the demand. The antiquarian John Aubrey, writing 'Of the Number of Attorneys in this County Now and Heretofore', reported that 'a hundred years since there were in the county of Gloucestershire but four attorneys, and now [1689] no fewer than three hundred attorneys and solicitors.' Thus there was legal work in the county for Robert Dover, drawing up leases, conveying property and representing his clients in London when they had a law case on hand.

Dover won the reputation of being a lawyer who tried to settle differences between people rather than urging them to go to the courts. The dashing Cavalier poet Sir William Davenant, thought by some to be the illegitimate son of Shakespeare, declared:

> Whilst Dover, that his knowledge not employs
> T'increase his neighbours quarrels, but their joys.

And at the end of this poem (which appears in the eighteenth-century reprint, not the original, of *Annalia Dubrensia*) a note is added: 'He was bred an attorney, who never tried but two causes: always made up the difference.'

By the time Dover moved to the country he was already married. His choice was Sibella Sanford, the daughter of a clergyman and Oxford college don who had retired to become rector of Lower Heyford in Oxfordshire. Sibella was the widow of a Bristol merchant, and she may also have been the author of the elaborate acrostic that is one of the poems in *Annalia Dubrensia*. If so she was a woman of educated tastes.

At some point after moving to Gloucestershire, Dover

started doing legal work for Endymion Porter, whose family was related to him by marriage. Porter, higher up the social scale than Dover, had attended Gray's Inn as a gentleman student some years after Dover had studied there, and his wife's cousins had been there at the same time as Dover. The Porter family estate at Aston sub Edge, about 650 acres, bordered on Weston sub Edge where the Dover Games were held.

Porter, a key person in the Olimpicks, spent most of his time in London at court. He started in the service of the Earl of Buckingham, then became Groom of the Bedchamber to Charles I. A patron of poets and playwrights including Sir William Davenant, he was Dover's link to the king. Porter was known to be enthusiastic about country games, so much so that the poet Robert Herrick, quite independently of Dover's poet friends, wrote a poem, 'The Country Life', addressed to Porter:

> For sports, for pageantry, and plays,
> Thou hast thy eves and holidays;
> On which the young men and maids meet
> To exercise their dancing feet;

Tripping the comely country round,
With daffodils and daisies crowned.
Thy wakes, thy quintals here thou hast,
Thy maypoles, too, with garlands graced;
Thy morris dance, thy Whitsun ale,
Thy shearing feast, which never fail.

Local tradition says that it was only a year after moving into Saintbury, just a little way away from the hill that was to take his name, that Dover started his Olimpick Games. Later he was to move into the village of Childswickham, a place within a short horse-ride of Dover's Hill.

Putting on some kind of country entertainment was common among gentry who could afford it, particularly at festival times or if there were royal visitors to amuse. Queen Anne, wife of James I, for instance, was entertained in Wiltshire with a 'pastoral'. The vicar took part dressed as a bard, with 'his parishioners in shepherds' weeds'. The pastoral was a 'song' in four parts, probably with music since the minister had 'made several of his parishioners good musicians, both for vocal and instrumental music'.

There was also a convention whereby such entertainments might be set in an ancient Greek landscape. The pastoral genre with Arcadian shepherds was popular in poetry. Edmund Spenser had written *The Shepheardes Calendar*, a highly influential poem in which he was one of the shepherds and wrote about his life as if it was that of a simple rustic.

Had Dover simply put on a few pastoral pageants, it would have been relatively unremarkable. Instead, in the Games he organised, real shepherds together with the local gentry re-enacted ancient Greek games – or so people came to believe. Most educated people knew about the Olympic Games, Shakespeare included. Though the playwright was reputed to have had little Latin and less Greek, he made a reference to the Olympic Games in one of his plays.

There are even two other brief references to Olympic or Olympian Games during the seventeenth century – on the Gog Magog hills outside Cambridge, and another at Hampton Court later in the century. But both of these descriptions appear in print later than the start of Dover's Olimpicks, and nothing more is heard of them. In contrast, Dover's Games became well known to his contemporaries. The idea of a re-enactment or an adaptation of the original Olympics attracted attention three centuries before the modern Olympic movement.

Why did Dover do it? Why did a country lawyer, from a family of the middling rather than the aristocratic kind, start the first ever English Olimpicks? Whatever gave him such a remarkable idea in the first place? What made his Cotswold Games so special?

Looking back after the Games had been going successfully

for several years, Robert Dover himself wasn't sure of his motives. As quoted before, he wrote:

> I cannot tell what planet ruled, when I
> First undertook this mirth, this jollity,
> Nor can I give account to you at all,
> How this conceit into my brain did fall.
> Or how I durst assemble, call together
> Such multitudes of people as come hither.

One of his motives was clearly just to have fun. The famous 'Dover Castle', a pun on the real thing in Kent, is proof of that. This was a portable wooden structure, which could be

put up on site each year and then dismantled and stored till the following year. Others, before Dover, had had the idea of building wooden devices for outdoor occasions. London pageants of the previous century often included castles with flying pennants. Sometimes these were erected on four-wheeled carts and pulled in a procession. Queen Elizabeth had watched a River Thames pageant with a 'goodly castle' in 1561, for instance.

But Dover's castle was unusual enough to delight and entrance the onlookers. It was not only designed to look like a castle, it also had small cannons which fired blanks with real gunpowder! The 'castle walls' are referred to in a way which suggests it was quite large, big enough for people to get inside it, and clearly it was strong enough to hold those small cannons. The various references to it show both the ingenuity and the joviality of the man who ordered it built.

The guns would have been set off by a person inside the castle lighting the gunpowder by means of a linstock, a pole with a smouldering cord clamped at the end. Presumably the cannons were mounted either on wheels or on slides, so that after being fired they could be withdrawn into the castle for reloading with powder down the muzzle.

The explosions were loud enough to impress the onlookers. They were poetically compared to 'the voice of angry Jove' and to 'thunder and lightning'. This elaborate joke required Dover to have royal permission for supplies of gunpowder, permission that was given by Charles I, presumably via Endymion Porter.

There's a charming picture of the castle in the frontispiece to *Annalia Dubrensia*, showing a cannon on either side and a pennant with a cross at the top blowing in the wind. The castle sits on a round pivot. 'It may have been based on the structure of a post mill, a type of windmill common in the seventeenth century,' says historian Matthew Alexander, who has made a special study of the castle.

In a post mill of this time, a strong central post is braced upright by four diagonal struts. A large metal pin at the top fits into a socket in the centre of a cross beam – rather like the top bar of a capital T. The mill structure hangs from this cross beam, and so can be turned in any direction to face the wind. None of this is shown in the illustration of Dover's Castle, which just depicts a drum-like base.

However it would have been well-known technology to carpenters of the time.

Dover's Castle captivated many of the poets who wrote about his Games. Its peaceful nature, its cannon-fire and its mobility (compared with real castles) were praised in the poems, often in mock heroic style. A poem by Richard Wells, presumably one of Dover's local friends, has this to say:

> Shall I blame
> Thy building castles in the air of Fame,
> Which will as long stand out as shall those hills,
> Against Time's envy, or time-pleasers' wills?
> Oh no, thy castle shall exceed as far
> Th' other Dover's as sweet peace doth war.

Yet a wooden castle, particularly one with working cannon, is hardly an idea borrowed from ancient Greece or the Olympic Games. Indeed, though Dover's friends made much of the comparison between ancient Olympia and the Cotswolds, Dover's Games were not rigidly formed on the Olympic pattern. His poem, the only explanation that we have directly from him unlike the other poems in the celebratory book, does not specifically compare his Games with the ancient Olympic ones, though he does refer to the good influence of games upon ancient Greece.

So Dover may not originally have started up his Games with the primary aim of re-enacting the ancient Olympics. The Dover Games' historian, Dr Francis Burns, suggests that this 'Olimpick' epithet originated with the poet Michael Drayton. Drayton contributed the first celebratory poem in *Annalia Dubrensia* which includes these lines:

> As those brave Grecians in their happy days,
> On Mount Olympus to their Hercules
> Ordained their games Olympic, and so named
> Of that great mountain; for those pastimes famed …
> Numbering their years, still their accounts they made
> Either from this or that Olympiad.
>   So Dover, from these games, by thee begun
> We'll reckon ours, as time away doth run.

Nevertheless, Dover's acquiescence in the term 'Olimpick' was wholehearted by 1636. For at the start of the book *Annalia Dubrensia*, published in that year, there is an epistle from the publisher, Matthew Walbancke, to Robert Dover, saying that although the ancient Olympics, founded by the legendary Hercules, are 'now utterly abandoned, and their memories almost extinguished', Dover, a hero of his age just as Hercules was a hero, had revived the memory of them. The comparison with the ancient Olympics is explicit. Dover must have been happy with this to let it stand.

The label 'Olimpick' would have offered him the advantage of obscuring any link with Catholicism, particularly if he had taken over and expanded a local church ale. For, as we have seen, the old church ales were linked with the pre-Protestant Catholic Church. A man like Dover, who had been brought up in the old religion, might well be wary of anything that would draw attention to this.

By letting his Games be called 'Olimpick', Dover secularised them. Olimpick Games were not, and could not be, church ales. Theirs was a pagan, not a church, model. Moreover, the classical term gentrified the sports. Educated men had heard of the Olympic Games; poor shepherds and farm workers would not have done so.

It is worth remembering that the book of the Games was published twenty or so years after they had started. The Latin title *Annalia Dubrensia* can be translated as the annals or yearly records of Dover. Yet this it is not. Instead it is a collection or anthology of thirty-four congratulatory verses about Dover and his Games, including a poem by Dover himself.

The poetry was, however, in the ancient Olympic tradition. The poet Pindar had written many odes celebrating the Olympic and other ancient games, and the celebrations at Olympia included victory hymns and odes specially commissioned from leading poets. So it is possible that Dover's book of poetry was a conscious imitation of ancient custom.

Annalia Dubrensia was also a seventeenth-century equivalent of an official book of prose celebrating today's modern Olympics. Nowadays poetry is a minority genre in publishing, but in the seventeenth century collections of poetry were part of the London publishing scene. Even prose books often started with two or three congratulatory poems addressed to the author. Some poets would contribute in return for pay. Gentleman amateurs would write a poem for friendship's sake. Almost anybody with a pretension to culture would be able to turn out some kind of poem. So many of Dover's relations, friends, lawyers and clergymen obliged with some verses.

Dover, however, included many good professional poets among his friends and neighbours. There were verses by well-known poets like Michael Drayton, Thomas Randolph, William Basse and Ben Jonson, as well as playwrights Shackerley Marmion and Thomas Heywood. And many of the other contributors were men of letters who had published prose works of some kind. Dover was a cultured man and, of course, his friend and employer Endymion Porter was closely involved with court amusements and thus with poets, playwrights and musicians.

The poems in Dover's book described, explained and justified his Games, and were designed to increase Dover's status as well as to celebrate the Games. The publisher Matthew Walbancke may have claimed that Dover was too modest to want the verses published, but this was a piece of polite fiction usual at the time. The book was also propaganda promoting the idea of Merry England against the Puritans.

Michael Drayton wrote the first poem that sets the scene for the Olimpick Games, both placing them in the pastoral literary tradition and making the comparison with the ancient Olympics. By opening the book with a poem by Drayton, Dover was putting the best first. Drayton is known to us today for the striking and beautiful sonnet, 'Since there's no help, come let us kiss and part'. But his contemporaries would also have known and respected him as the author of a much longer pastoral poem, *Poly-Olbion,* which is a kind of poetic journey around England and Wales.

Poly-Olbion, epic in length if not subject matter, contains a description of the Cotswolds, the town of Evesham and a nearby hill, maybe even Dover's Hill, 'where little purling winds like wantons seem to dally'. Charming seventeenth-century woodcuts illustrated some poetic lines about a shepherds' celebration, showing them grouped round a pole flying a flag with the message 'Heigh for Cotswold'. The influence of this poem is evident in some of the other poetry in Dover's book.

Drayton would have known about Dover's Games because he spent two or three months each summer at the home of his patron, Sir Henry Rainsford, who lived at Clifford Chambers near Stratford-upon-Avon. It was while he was there that he wrote *Poly-Olbion* and he probably attended the Dover Games. As he died five years before Dover's book was actually published, it is clear that the various poems were collected over several years. Getting him to write a poem about the Games was not unlike getting a celebrity author's endorsement today.

The other major poet in Dover's book was Ben Jonson. His

was a dissenting voice among the other poets, who were happy to pick up the Olimpick theme from Drayton. He wrote a short and slightly grudging poem in which he says he cannot bring himself to compare the Games with the original Olympics, calling them merely the 'great Instauration of his Hunting and Dancing at Cotswold'. According to the antiquarian John Aubrey, 'King James made him [Ben Jonson] write against the Puritans.' In his poem Jonson claims that the Games 'renew the glories of our blessed James' and 'keep alive his memory' – an example of how the Games began to be seen as gesture of loyalty to the king.

Naturally Dover himself comes in for a lot of light-hearted praise in his book! Perhaps the most delightful tribute comes from Nicholas Wallington, whose poem is titled 'To the Great Inventor and Champion of English Olimpicks, Pythicks, Nemicks, Isthmicks; the great architect and Engineer of the famous and admirable Portable Fabric of Dover Castle, her Ordnance and Artillery, and the true voice of Himself, his Games, Mirth, Fortification'.

What stops the praise being over the top is the playful tone, making it clear that the more preposterous compliments are part of the fun. It includes these charming lines:

Diana with her nymphs did bless his birth;
His mother daughter was to goddess Mirth,
Who did him swaddle in her lily smock,
And Queen of Fairies made his cradle rock;
King Oberon did him dandle in his arms;
Pug [Puck] sang 'By-Baby' with delightful charms.

Jonson apart, most of the poets followed the comparison with the ancient Olympics, likening Dover with Hercules, traditional founder of the Greek games. Although other famous Greek games – Pythian, Nemian and Isthmian – are mentioned, the Olympic comparison is the predominant theme. Some of the later poets refer to the earlier poems, suggesting that they had read other contributions before making their own.

Thomas Randolph, the poet and playwright, who died a year before Dover's book was published, took the opportunity to lament the passing of the old church ales, morris dances and country games like Barley-break, and to blame Puritans for reducing the fun in the world.

> These teach that dancing is a Jezebel
> And Barley-break the ready way to hell;
> The morris, idols; Whitsun ales can be
> But profane relics of a Jubilee!

Another theme was the peaceful and well-behaved nature of the occasion – putting distance between Dover's Games and the traditional drunken church ales attended by villagers, not gentry. His brother-in-law, William Cole, claimed that Dover could 'civilise the untuned swain', while Ferriman Rutter, a clergyman who had never attended the Games, wrote:

> Such good decorum in thy mirth to be,
> In such a concourse, such a company;
> Such honest mirth, and company so fair,
> No oaths, nor curses to infect the air;
> No fightings, quarrels – as I hear report –
> Makes it more lawful; thee admired for't.

To make sure of the good decorum, Robert Dover's Games were firmly under his control. 'Dover was constantly there in person well mounted and accoutred, and was the chief director and manager of those games frequented by the nobility and gentry (some of whom came 60 miles to see them)', according to Anthony à Wood. A picture shows him with a wand of office (or perhaps just a riding stick) mounted upon what is probably a white horse, an equine symbol of his authority.

Dover produced the equivalent of a modern logo – his own favours. These were knots or straight pieces of ribbon that could be pinned on a hat, tied on the arm (like a black mourning band today), put on the leg like a garter or even worn round the neck. His favours were well known in the county and could be worn long after the Games had ceased. Ferriman Rutter wrote of recognising Dover's favour out hunting – 'when I see thy yearly favour – yellow, worn in thy huntsman's cap'. The choice of this bright colour may have been significant – some Puritans thought yellow a 'light wanton colour'.

In the hard agricultural world of the seventeenth century even the gift of a ribbon would have value to a villager. But as well as handing out favours, Dover gave out prizes. Valuable silver items were awarded for the mounted sports, to be returned yearly by the gentry. His picture shows him

carrying a bag, probably a money bag. This may mean the shepherds and workers who took part in the backsword and gymnastic sports were given prizes of money.

There was also feasting. The frontispiece to Dover's book shows ten men, but curiously no women, at a table outside the castle. But it wasn't just the gentry who were fed. It is Wallington again who mentions that Dover made sure that the lower sort of men and women got fed too:

He spares no cost; this also doth afford
To those that sit at any lower board.
None ever hungry from these Games come home,
Or e'er made plaint of viands, or of room.

In this and other poems there was a suggestion that the Games may function as a way of bringing together rich and poor and creating social harmony. John Stratford, Dover's relation by marriage, wrote:

Thy sport are merely harmless, such they be,
Augment the bond of love and unity.

Perhaps this deal of social harmony through sport was one reason why Robert Dover's Olimpicks caught the public imagination. So famous were the Cotswold lawyer and his Games that his name was given to a town thousands of miles away in the New World. Dover, a historic former mill town in New Hampshire, was incorporated with its name in 1641, and some people since have suggested its name came from the port in Kent. But according to *New Hampshire Town Names and Whence They Came* by Elmer

Munson Hunt, 'The name appears to have been taken from Robert Dover (1575–1641), English soldier and lawyer and founder of the "Cotswold Games", originated in protest against the growing severity of Puritanism at the time.'

There could be no greater compliment to the new Olimpicks.

TO MY NOBLE FRIEND
Mr Robert Dover
ON HIS BRAVE ANNUAL ASSEMBLIES
UPON COTSWOLD

As those brave Grecians in their happy days,
On Mount Olympus to their Hercules
Ordained their games Olympic, and so named
Of that great mountain; for those pastimes famed:
Where then their able youth leapt, wrestled, ran,
Threw the armed dart; and honoured was the man
That was the victor; in the circuit there
The nimble rider, and skilled charioteer
Strove for the garland; in those noble times
There to their harps the poets sang their rhymes;
That, whilst Greece flourished, and was only then
Nurse of all arts, and of all famous men;
Numb'ring their years, still their accounts they made,
Either from this or that Olympiad.

    So Dover, from these games, by thee begun,
We'll reckon ours, as time away doth run.
We'll have thy statue in some rock cut out,
With brave inscriptions garnishèd about,
And under written: 'Lo, this was the man,
Dover, that first these noble sports began.'

MICHAEL DRAYTON

Chapter 3

MANLY SPORTS
AND THE
First Olympic Contests

Dover's Games claimed to be based on the original Olympic Games of ancient Greece. 'Cotswold sports, where each Olimpick Game is paralleled,' wrote William Denny, a poet and contemporary of Dover's at Gray's Inn. But a closer examination shows that this was only partly true. Not only did Dover's Olimpicks take place yearly, unlike the four-year cycle of the original Olympics, but not all of the sports on the Cotswold hillside were Olympian in nature, just as many of the modern Olympic sports are unlike those of the ancient world.

The games of ancient Olympia included foot races, foot racing in full armour, wrestling (both ordinary and all-in wrestling), boxing, horse races, mule cart races and chariot races. The ancient Greeks also invented the pentathlon, a five-part contest consisting of throwing the discus, throwing the javelin, jumping, running and wrestling.

We have the frontispiece and the poems of *Annalia Dubrensia* to tell us which sports were practised on Kingcombe Plain. One immediate difference between Dover's Games and the originals is what the athletes were wearing. All the Cotswolds athletes are dressed in doublet and hose (like knee-length socks or longer ones like stockings), with baggy breeches to knee level. While the ancient Greeks competed naked, there is no sign from this picture that Dover's young men even took their doublets off.

The seventeenth-century sports were performed in a culture that was very different from that of ancient Greece,

where attendance at the gymnasium was part of an educated man's lifestyle. In traditional Christianity, whether Catholic or Protestant, the body was innately inferior to the mind or the soul. The health of a man's soul was of much more concern than the health of his body.

True, the idea of sport as part of a healthy lifestyle wasn't completely foreign to the seventeenth century. In a society in which educated men read the classical authors, it couldn't be. In *The Anatomy of Melancholy,* a rambling masterpiece

on the topic of mental depression, Robert Burton quotes these Greek and Latin authorities at length, listing all the various exercises, games and recreations which might help men fight off melancholy and explaining: 'Riches may not easily be had without labour and industry, nor learning without study, neither can our health be preserved without bodily exercise.'

There was also a growing body of literature about education, and in this could be found the idea that sport was a necessity for boys as a way of promoting health. In 1581, Richard Mulcaster, head of St Paul's School in London, wrote: 'But now what place hath exercise here? … To defend the body by defeating diseases?' His book, *Positions,* could be said to be one of the first English books about athletics, claiming: 'All exercises were first devised, and so indeed served, either for games and pastime, for war and service, or for surety of health and length of life, though sometime all the three ends did concur in one.'

It was as a preparation for war, rather than as an aid to health, that sports were legitimised in seventeenth-century society. Ordinary working men, not just gentleman schoolboys, should be allowed to take part because, Burton argues in *The Anatomy of Melancholy*, the sports 'hath in former times been enjoined by statute as a defensive exercise and an honour to our land, as well may witness our victories in France.'

Warlike sports included anything from athletic exercises (important for keeping soldiers fit) to bloodthirsty contests in which men could be seriously injured or even killed. The modern term for these would be martial arts. 'These were primarily military arts used secondarily as sports,' says Terry Brown of the Company of Maisters. He is a historian, practitioner and teacher of English martial arts including bare-fist fighting, backswording and quarterstaffing. 'When I teach them I teach them as I would have in the seventeenth century, not as sports but as martial arts. These were fighting systems which could be used as sports, not sports that could be used as fighting systems. They are incredibly skilful and incredibly vicious.'

Seventeenth-century fights, whether for sport or anger, often resulted in maiming or death. In a fight between Sir German Poole and a Mr Hutchinson of Gray's Inn, Robert Dover's old law school, Poole cut off three of Hutchinson's fingers before he had even drawn his sword. In revenge

Hutchinson sliced off Poole's nose, picked it up, pocketed it and went off with it so that it could not be sewn on again. It was the mean attitude in taking away the slice of nose, not the fact that it was cut off in the first place, which made this particular sword contest the subject of gossip!

Every man, other than the poor, wore a sword. It was vital for personal protection on unlit streets where there was no police force at all. John Aubrey noted that in 1673 he had been

> in danger of being run through with a sword by a young Templer at Mr Burges' chamber in the Middle Temple. The year that I lay at Mr Never's for a short time I was in great danger of being killed by a drunkard in the street of Gray's Inn Gate by a gentleman whom I never saw before but, *deo gratias*, one of his companions hindered his thrust.

A sword was also part of a gentleman's dress for formal occasions. The picture of Robert Dover at his Olimpick Games shows him with his sword hanging from his shoulder.

Ironically the seventeenth century's bloodthirsty attitude to fighting sports was closer to the spirit of the original Olympics than the safety-conscious attitude of today. In ancient Olympic boxing contests, although wrestling holds were banned, almost any blow anywhere was permissible. One contestant died when a jab under his ribs tore out his entrails.

But though there is a mention of the powerful fist of a 'war-like champion' in one of the relatively early poems in *Annalia Dubrensia*, it is not clear whether Robert Dover's Games included bare-fist boxing, for it is unlikely (though not impossible) that the wrestling contests included fist blows. There is no picture of this in the frontispiece. If it was a sport originally included in the Games, then it may have been dropped later when approval was sought from or given by King James.

For King James listed the sports he thought suitable for his son and heir in *Basilicon Doron*: 'The exercises that I would have you to use (although but moderately, not making a craft of them) are running, leaping, wrestling, fencing, dancing, and playing at the catch or tennis, archery, palle maille, and such like other faire and pleasant field games.' Bare-fist fighting was not among these legitimate sports.

Wrestling, on the other hand, was definitely practised up on Kingcombe Plain – the king had given his approval to this. A charming picture in *Annalia Dubrensia* shows two men in doublet and breeches in a wrestling stance. Some have interpreted this picture as showing a shin-kicking contest – a vicious rural sport that featured in the later Cotswold Olimpicks. But *Annalia Dubrensia* is absolutely clear that it was wrestling, not mere shin-kicking, which was held at the Games. This was what Richard Mulcaster, the schoolmaster author of *Positions*, called 'upright wrestling'.

(This distinction was important since the original Olympics included pancratical wrestling, a vicious contest with few rules where strangling was allowed and only gouging and biting were banned.)

Not only did wrestling have specific royal approval, it had been one of the court entertainments put on for Christian of Denmark, King James' brother-in-law, when he visited his sister, James' queen. Moreover, it could be legitimised by the Bible episode in Genesis when Jacob wrestles with a stranger who turns out to be God himself. If God had wrestled, then wrestling must be permitted to man!

The ring for a wrestling contest was usually created by the onlookers linking arms. The contestants tried to over-throw each other, clasping each other by the arm or neck. The loser was the man whose upper body touched the ground first, and there were probably three bouts per fight.

Shin-kicking, as well as hooking your opponent's legs, was a legitimate tactic within wrestling, and it was only later that it became a specialised sport of its own. 'Shin-kicking weakens the wrestler's stance,' explains Terry Brown, author of *English Martial Arts*. 'Sometimes wrestlers even fought in wooden clogs. There is a story that one wrestler walked home so bruised that even a blade of grass was painful to his legs.'

The question of whether a gentleman should take part in country games was discussed as early as 1561 in *The Courtier*, an Italian etiquette book translated by Thomas Hoby. One character in the book maintained that in Lombardy

> you will see there young gentlemen upon the holy days come dance all the day long in the sun with them of the country, and pass the time with them in casting the bar, in wrestling, running and leaping. And I believe it is not ill done. For no comparison is there made of nobleness of birth, but of force and slight, in which things many times the men of the country are not a whit inferior to a gentleman, and it seemeth this familiar conversation containeth in it a certain lovely freeness.

However, the argument against this was also put by another character who maintained: 'It is too ill a sight and too foul a matter and without estimation to see a gentleman overcome by a carter and especially in wrestling.'

So did the local gentry take part in the wrestling bouts on Kingcombe Plain? Probably not. While a young prince or a gentleman might, as King James had suggested, enjoy wrestling as part of a programme of warlike arts and general fitness, he was expected to do so 'moderately, not making a craft' of it. So it is likely that the wrestlers came from the local villagers, shepherds and household or stable staff of the gentry.

Writing in the early years of the following century, in 1714, Sir Thomas Parkyns, who had learned his wrestling techniques at Dover's old *alma mater*, Gray's Inn, complained that wrestling was no longer practised by the gentry. 'If wrestling was more practised by gentlemen, etc., few or none would be killed by the sword,' he thought.

Parkyns described wrestling contests between working men at church ales, with the village girls looking on. 'For the most part our country rings for wrestlings, at wakes and other festivals, consist of a small party of young women, who come not hither to choose a coward, but the daring, healthy and robust persons fit to raise an offspring from,' he writes encouragingly, though he was not sure even village girls would approve of 'the rending and tearing of waistcoats, kicking and breaking of shins'.

Another sport was throwing the sledge or hammer. This, it could be argued, was a seventeenth-century version of the Olympic sport of discus-throwing or today's shot-putting. But it was not one of the sports recommended by King James for his son. Nor did Henry Peacham, author of *The Compleat Gentleman* in 1620, think much of it. 'For the throwing [of weights] and wrestlings, I hold them exercises not so well beseeming nobility, but rather soldiers in a camp, or a prince's guard ...' So it is likely that the sledge-throwing contests of Dover's Games were practised by the village men rather than the gentry's sons.

There was also spurning – or throwing or casting – the bar. This sport, the equivalent of tossing the caber in today's Highland games, was beginning to lose its gentility. Once it had been the sport of kings. Henry VIII, even after his accession to the throne, would enjoy himself spurning the bar, but now it had

slid down the social scale and was a sport for the lower orders. Usually the bar was a long heavy wooden pole, but the game could also be played with pikes.

As pike-throwing, it became a legitimate part of military training. Prince Henry, the elder son of King James I, who died young, had taken a special interest in military matters and had used pike-tossing as part of his martial keep-fit programme. In the illustration of Dover's Games, there are two men each clearly throwing a long pole, and there is just a suggestion of a pointed tip to each. This could mean they were hurling pikes rather than poles, though the poems make no reference to pikes.

Also in the illustration are two men with shorter poles in a vertical position. Interestingly, these instruments are neither being thrown nor being wielded as weapons. In the opinion

of English martial arts expert Terry Brown, these men may be spurning (as opposed to throwing or casting) the bar 'because the illustration very clearly demonstrates that one of the men is supporting the bottom of the bar on his foot. Spurning relates to kicking or pushing with the foot.'

But it may be significant that both men are wearing hats – whereas all the participants in the sports, other than the horse riders, are bare-headed. It seems possible, therefore, that these two are sticklers. These were umpires who gave their name to the phrase 'a stickler for the rules'. 'Sticklers carried sticks to part a sword fight safely,' Terry Brown explains. 'You can't just get in there and separate swordsmen. Even if they were fighting with wooden swords, you'd get badly hurt.'

Sword play was an important part of Dover's Olimpicks. The illustration shows two men fighting with sword and dagger in the then modern way. A century earlier, sword play would have been with sword and buckler, a kind of shield, but bucklers had fallen out of fashion. They were heavy weapons to take on journeys. A dagger was easier to carry around and could be used as an offensive as well as a defensive weapon to parry a blow.

But even this kind of sword play was going out of fashion among the smart set. By the seventeenth century the use of the rapier, a slim thrusting blade, instead of a wide sword, both a thrusting and a slashing weapon, was gaining ground. While Robert Dover is shown riding his horse with a broadsword by his side, some of the more dashing Cavaliers at the Games would have been wearing the slender narrow rapier.

Writing in 1599 George Silver, author of *Paradoxes of Defence*, lamented the loss of the old broadsword or backsword. With a positive zeal for blood-letting, he claimed that the rapier was the inferior weapon because it did less damage. A slashing blow from a sword, however,

> being strongly made, taketh sometimes clean away the hand from the arm, hath many times been seen. Again a full blow upon the head or face with a short sharp sword is most commonly death. A full blow upon the neck, shoulder, arm or leg, endangereth life, cutteth off the veins, muscles, and sinews, perisheth the bones; these wounds made by the blow, in respect of perfect healing, are the loss of limbs, or maims incurable for ever.

The thrusts of the newfangled rapier, on the other hand, 'being made through the hand, arm or leg, or in many places of the body and face, are not deadly, neither are they maims, or loss of limbs or life'. Nor did Silver approve of the new fashion of fighting with sword and dagger rather than sword and buckler, claiming that the dagger was much less effective at defence than the buckler. 'The dagger is an imperfect ward ...'

What the illustrations cannot show is whether these swords and daggers were metal or wooden weapons. The figures in the illustration are fighting with closed or enclosed hilts, designed to shield the hand, and at first sight this looks as if this must mean metal weapons. But these hilts could be made out of wickerwork or leather, and slid on to wooden cudgels. On wooden swords they are called 'pots'.

Wooden weapons, rather than metal ones, seem more likely if Dover was anxious to promote relatively harmless sports – though it is possible, even likely, that the word 'harmless' refers to spiritual rather than physical harmlessness. We know that such contests were part of the traditional church ales and wakes, sometimes being called cudgel play, at other times called single sticks or backswording. Robert Herrick's poem 'The Wake' says:

> Near the dying of the day,
> There will be a cudgel-play,
> Where a coxcomb will be broke
> Ere a good word can be spoke.

The 'coxcomb' of the poem was the jokey word for the head. 'The rules were often best of three with the bout being decided by "breaking the head" i.e. by drawing blood on the head,' says Terry Brown, one of the few men to practise cudgel play today. Strict rules required an inch of blood to be visible. 'Players nonetheless deliberately targeted other parts of the body in order to try and bring down the guard of the opponent and thereby cause him to leave the head unguarded and open to scoring blows. It's a hard sport.' A cudgel blow can easily break an arm.

The other reason for thinking the weapons were wooden is that both fighters are holding their weapons high. 'With a wooden sword contest, if the winner is the first to draw blood on the head, then you would be protecting the head most of all. Because only a blow on the head, not one on the body, would count,' points out Terry Brown. And if the weapons were wooden, the likelihood is that the contestants were not gentlemen. While sword play was undoubtedly part of the education of a gentleman, who might train with wooden weapons, public contests of cudgel play with wooden swords were not.

Even sword play with real swords was unlikely to be performed in a public contest by gentlemen. Later in the century, sword play contests were fought by professional swordsmen in public exhibitions. The reward was money thrown into the ring by the well-off onlookers. The contestants at the Cotswold Olimpicks, whether fighting with wooden or with metal swords, were probably rewarded in the same way

either by the better-off onlookers or by a cash prize from Dover's money bag.

But the shepherds, ploughboys and other farm workers, who fought with old-fashioned backswords and cudgels, would not necessarily be inferior to gentlemen in their skill and endurance. Indeed, sometimes they might even fight better than those who had gone to the newfangled rapier schools, according to George Silver.

Our ploughmen by nature will do all these things with great strength and agility: but the schoolman [i.e. a person taught at a newfangled school] is altogether unacquainted with these things. He being fast tied to such schoolplay as he hath learned, hath lost thereby the benefit of nature, and the ploughman is now by nature without art a far better man than he ...

There is no manner of teaching comparable to the old ancient teaching, that is, first their quarters, then their wards, blows, thrusts, and breaking of thrusts, then their closes and grips, striking with the hilts, daggers, bucklers, wrestlings, striking with the foot or knee in the cods.

Less bloodthirsty and definitely in the ancient Olympic pattern were the athletic sports of running and leaping. These were considered useful for general fitness. 'Running is both a good exercise and a laudable solace,' wrote Sir Thomas Elyot, one of the early authors on education and exercise and author of *The Book named The Governor* in 1531. There were classical precedents. Anybody who had looked into Homer's epic *Iliad* – and most educated men had done so either in the original Greek or in a translation – knew that its hero, Achilles, was described as 'swift footed'.

'To running I add leaping and jumping,' wrote James Cleland, giving various examples from the ancient Greeks in *The Institution of a Young Noble Man* in 1607. He had been tutor to a friend of Prince Henry's, King James' older son, so he followed King James' line, arguing that taking part in a public contest was not suitable for noblemen. 'Alexander [the Great] being a child excelled all his companions in running. Who being demanded on a time to run at the great game Olympus, answered wisely, that he could have run very gladly, had there been any kings' – meaning that he refused to compete against his social inferiors.

Headmaster Richard Mulcaster, in *Positions*, warned of the dangers of leaping to those with gout or swollen veins in the leg. He pointed out that in the ancient world leaping was useful 'in warfare to skip over ditches and hard passages'. He added, rather mysteriously, that 'skipping against the bank', though it might hurt the breast, would help the hips and that 'the same downhill cleareth the head'. Had Dover read Mulcaster's book? Or is it mere chance that the man shown leaping in the frontispiece illustration is leaping down, rather than up, the hill?

So the contestants for running, jumping and doing a headstand were probably shepherds or ploughboys rather than gentlemen's sons, who should not be seen competing against their social inferiors. Running and leaping had the approval of King James for his son but 'only moderately, not making a craft of them'. As for headstands, the king added, 'I debar ... such tumbling tricks as only serve for comedians and balladines [acrobats] to win their bread with.' The man in doublet and breeches shown standing on his head in the *Annalia Dubrensia* would not have had royal approval.

Social class and sport, from the days of Alexander the Great onwards and perhaps before, have often had an uneasy relationship. The seventeenth-century attitude was the exact opposite to that of Victorian sports enthusiasts, who laid down a rule for the first modern Olympics that only amateurs could compete – a rule that meant the early English athletes tended to be public schoolboys rather than the sons and daughters of poorer families.

This complete dichotomy between the seventeenth and nineteenth century on the class question led to other differences too. If only the unlettered could compete, then sporting contests of wrestling, athletics and sword play were essentially low status. The victors could be rewarded with money, but they could not become inspirational figures, like today's sports heroes or like the original Olympic winners who were immortalised in verse and marble. Not a single winner at any of the events was thought worth naming in *Annalia Dubrensia*.

Nor are scores or time records noted in any of the poems. The technology to do so barely existed. Portable watches (in boxes or hung from the belt) had been invented in the sixteenth century but were rare, costly and relatively unreliable devices unsuitable for the business of competitive time-keeping. Even so, had the will to do so been there, it might have been possible to time events using a marked candle, an hourglass with sand like the traditional egg timer, or even a water clock. Such devices, after all, were used on board ship to tell the time.

But nobody in Dover's time was much interested in sports record-keeping or record-breaking. It is not till 1663, years after the death of Robert Dover and in the days of Charles II, that there is mention of public interest in a foot race between a famous runner and the Duke of Richmond's footman – and then the interest was in betting on the outcome rather than recording time and distance run.

And without the interest in competition records, there could be no incentive (had it been possible) for the Cotswold

Olimpicks to make a link with other sporting events or to develop some sort of national, rather than local, significance. The highly developed competitiveness of the modern Olympics with records of all kinds could not exist three centuries ago.

Probably the running champion displayed his prowess at other local church ales, if the races had prizes worth winning and if he could get time off from his employer to do so. The sword-play champion at the Dover Games might have done a little better. With his reputation enhanced by winning, he might even have had employment offers for passing on his skill to others. And there was going to be, in the future, a demand for good swordsmen. His skill and his endurance would be needed not for sporting contests but for real war.

AN ECONOMIASTICK
TO HIS WORTHY FRIEND
Mr Robert Dover
ON HIS FAMOUS ANNUAL ASSEMBLIES
AT COTSWOLD

Each huntsman there, with skill and hope, brings forth
His best bred dogs, to show their ablest worth …
The swallow-footed greyhound hath the prize,
A silver-studded collar, who outflies
The rest in lightning's speed, who first comes by
His straining copes-mates, with celerity
Turns his affrighted game, then cotes again
His forward rival, on the senseless plain,
And after labyrinthian turns, surprise
The game, whilst he doth pant her obsequies;
    Then by and by, swift racing nags contend
Who first shall message conquest to the end
Of their appointed course. At first begin
All equal in their steps and hope to win,
And Fortune hides her favourite from the eye
Of each beholder and joyed rider, by
Some mile, till one that scorns rivality
Blushing at this so long equality,
Loosens his hard-born reins, and then most cry,
Proclaiming him the hope of victory.

WILLIAM DENNY

[92]

Chapter 4

GENTLEMEN'S SPORTS
AND A
Classical Theme

Though many of the sports closest to those of the ancient Greek games involved the Cotswold villagers rather than the gentry, on their own they would not have been enough to interest the surrounding landowners and professional people, despite the label of 'Olimpick'. Yet Dover provided contests and entertainments that persuaded the local gentry to travel up to sixty miles – a long haul in the days of horse transport and amazingly bad roads.

For the better-off he put on horse racing, hunting and

coursing. Of these only the horse racing could be said to be an ancient Olympic sport. But by adding coursing and hunting to horse racing, Dover made his Olimpicks far more attractive to the gentry. Today we have forgotten the importance of the horse. Like today's car, a horse was not just a necessity for travel, it was also a cherished possession, a source of speed and enjoyment, and a sign of status.

Seventeenth-century aristocrats, like the Earl of Pembroke, had as many as a hundred horses in their stables – war horse, race horses, early Arabs known as Moroccans, carriage horses for half a dozen coaches, hunters, and ordinary hacks for getting around. Local gentlemen like Dover, a professional man but not an aristocrat, would have had riding horses and horses that pulled the carriages bringing the elderly or the womenfolk to the Games.

So the equine events were those in which the local land-owners might compete personally. Even in the horse racing, where some of the horses were probably ridden not by the owners but by grooms or stable staff, the sons of local land-owners also probably took part for fun, rather as they still do today in local point-to-points. Horsemanship was an essential for the would-be gentleman. King James I, in his book of advice for his son, declared: 'the honourablest and most commendable games that ye can use, are on horseback: for it becometh a prince best of any man, to be a fair and good horseman.'

And, of course, horse events were not part of the usual church ales. By adding them to his Games, Dover transformed a peasant celebration into one for people of position. Racing was becoming the sport of kings, and Robert Dover would have known that racing had the support of the monarchy. One of the congratulatory poems even suggested that the Dover Games might one day outstrip the race meetings at Royston and Newmarket, both places patronised by

King James and King Charles I, where there were proper race courses and royal hunting boxes. The Games already overshadowed the racing at Brackley, Banstead and Salisbury (Sarum), claimed Walton Poole, another of Dover's friends from Gray's Inn:

> Shoot from thy firey fort,
> That Brackley may strike sail at thy report!
> Banstead and Sarum all their glory yield
> To thy Olimpicks sports, and give the field
> To more famed Cotswold.

In the poem by Thomas Randolph, which is a dialogue between two literary shepherds, there is a mention of the winner of the horse race at the Dover Games. It suggests that he was a gentleman, rather than a groom:

> a noble swain
> That spurred his spriteful palfrey o'er the plain,
> His head with ribbands crowned, and decked as gay
> As any lass upon her bridal day.

As well as ribbons there was also a miniature silver castle, possibly a salt-cellar, in the shape of Dover's own portable castle, as a prize for the winner.

How long was the course? The poet William Denny describes a gruelling race:

> Then some with switches urge their utmost speed,
> And others' spurs are bathed in flanks that bleed …
> Whiles one that sears his almost sinking horse,
> With switch and spur, doth labour on the course!

Today the course has vanished under ploughed fields, so it is no longer possible to trace its length, but posters for the Games in the nineteenth century speak of two and a quarter miles. In those days the races were run in a series of three heats, which suggests it was a relatively narrow course, reducing the number of horses that could start at one time.

In the frontispiece to *Annalia Dubrensia*, there are three men galloping on horseback and the back half of one horse in the lead disappearing off the left-hand edge of the page. This is probably the horse race. The riders are wearing hats and carry long poles which are probably riding sticks, the equivalent of today's riding crop. Similar ones, pointing up rather than down like today's crop, are carried by riders in contemporary woodcuts.

Also visible in the frontispiece are the hunting and coursing scenes. Hunting and coursing were a wise choice for Robert Dover if he wanted the approval of James I. The monarch, mad keen on the sport, often neglected his kingly duties to go hunting. On the way down from Scotland to take possession of the English throne, he hunted as he went. In April at Burleigh, 'before his coming there were prepared train-scents; and live hares in baskets being carried to the heath, made excellent sport for his Majesty, all the way betwixt Sir John Harrington's and Stamford, Sir J.'s hounds

with good mouths following the game, the King taking great leisure and pleasure in the same.'

Actually supplying captured animals to hunt seems barbarous to most of us now, but in Jacobean England capturing a hare or a fox, then letting it out to be hunted, was acceptable sporting behaviour. The hares for the Games must have been previously caught then released on the hillside, for finding wild prey on a hillside swarming with onlookers would have been almost impossible. And, thanks to the illustration that shows two hares, separately pursued, we know that the greyhounds and the harriers hunted live prey, not a 'train-scent' (as in a drag hunt where the hounds pursue a scented trail, not a living creature).

What probably occurred on Dover Hill is a variation of 'paddock hunting'. For this form of sport a strip of grassland would be enclosed by fences, and the prey, usually a deer, would be released at one end a little before the hounds. When the terrified beast had gone a certain distance, the hounds would be released for the chase. In the same county as Dover's Hill is a seventeenth-century hunting establishment called Lodge Park, near Aldsworth. It was built in 1635 next to a paddock hunting course, so that the gentlemen and ladies could amuse themselves with the spectacle of a deer chased to its death within the closed paddock. When not in use by its landowner, the course was rented out to the local gentry, at the price of ten shillings a deer, half a crown for each dog used, and twelve pence (a shilling) to the man who slipped their leash. Elaborate rules laid down which dogs won and provided for gambling on the results.

Robert Dover may have arranged something similar, using hares instead of deer, for his Games. When the hare was released, even without fencing, its trajectory could to a certain extent be organised by arranging where spectators stood. In this way, onlookers as well as riders could enjoy the chase.

From the illustrations on this page we can see that there were two kinds of hounds, both chasing hares. One couple are greyhounds, and these are chasing the hare by sight. The other group look like harriers or foxhounds, and they clearly are hunting by scent for two of them have their noses to the ground. The latter may have been Dover's own pack of hounds.

Though a hare was less noble a quarry than a deer, hunting it required knowledge and skill.

As for the hare, she has divers flights, as her win-
nowings and doublings, therefore at every default
give your hounds scope and leisure in casting about
for the windings of your rings, observing before she
swuats, her leaps and skips, bending to a place the
most likely to shelter her, for being reduced to such
shifts, she is at her last cast, and can no longer hold
out,

advised *The Young Sportsman's Instructor* of 1620.

Then as now, hunting was the sport of not just the rich
but also the aristocratic or would-be aristocratic. Naturally
James I recommended it highly to his son and heir. 'Hunting,

namely with running hounds ... is the most honourable and noblest sort' of games on horseback thereof; for it is a thievish form of hunting to shoot with guns and bows; and greyhound hunting is not so martial a game'.

Just as hunters cost more than ordinary hacks so a pack of hounds or even a kennel of greyhounds were expensive. Few gentlemen hunted (i.e. controlled and directed from horseback) their own hounds and thus, as well as kennel staff, a huntsman would be employed. Ferriman Rutter mentions meeting Dover's huntsman – 'when I see thy yearly favour – yellow, worn in thy huntsman's cap ...'

True enthusiasts, enjoyed the 'music', the baying of a pack in full cry, and chose their hounds partly for their voices. 'If you would have your kennel for sweetness of cry then you must compound it of some large dogs that have deep solemn mouths ... which must, as it were, bear the bass in the consort; then a double number of roaring and mouths, which must bear the counter tenor; then some hollow plain sweet mouths, which must bear the main or middle part; and so with these three parts of music you shall make your cry perfect,' advised sports expert Gervase Markham.

One of the poems in *Annalia Dubrensia* mentions the pack 'whose shrill-mouthed music, echoing, resounds' while soft-hearted poet William Basse even suggested that the hounds were valued for 'how they cried, not what they killed'. The harriers on the hillside would have had traditional names like the ones in Shakespeare's plays – Mountain, Fury, Tyrant, Ringwood, Sowler, Merriman, Clowder, Echo, Silver, Belman and Brabbler. Rich aristocratic hunting enthusiasts had several kinds of hounds – harbourers, big hounds used like today's tufters to seek out stags in their lying-up places; bulldogs, used when a stag was standing at bay; fox hounds, harriers and tumblers, which were small greyhounds or lurchers. There was even a 'slug' (i.e. sleuth) hound, a kind of bloodhound, brought down from Scotland by the king when he came to London.

There were bestselling hunting advice books, such as *The Young Sportsman's Instructor* of 1620. These books passed on, from one generation to another, the traditional lore of hunting, advising how to exercise the hounds and keep them in good health. The greyhounds at the Olimpicks probably ate better than the poorer villagers among the onlookers. Their ordinary food, according to Gervase Markham, included

'chippings, crusts of bread, soft tender bones or gristles of veal, lamb or such like, first scalded in beef broth not very salt, or any other broth that hath been boiled, mutton, veal or venison, or any kind of pullen, or for want thereof clean scalding water'. Before a match they would be given oatmeal and wheat mixed with aniseed and liquorice, whites of eggs, ale and balm, baked into loaves, and perhaps a boiled sheep's head.

One reason for the general approval of hunting was because it was warlike. 'Your body is disposed to endure patiently heat, rain, wind, cold, hunger and thirst; your mind made void of all idle and naughty cogitations,' wrote James Cleland.

It maketh a man courageous and valiant, in his enterprises: it teacheth him the situation of mountains, plains, the courses of brooks, and rivers. How am I able to reckon, the surprises, the stratagems, used for the obtaining of victory, according to the beasts you do hunt, which all are requisite and employed without difference at the wars, the hunting of men; for at them both your whole endeavours are to take, or kill.

Women enjoyed it too. A courtier reported of the old Queen Elizabeth at the age of seventy-seven: 'Her majesty is well and excellently disposed to hunting for every second day she is on horseback, and continues the sport long.' Quite often the most noble person at a hunt was the one who gave the deer the final knife or arrow thrust that ended its life.

But it was coursing, the hunting of the hare by grey-hounds, not harriers, that was thought most suitable for the ladies or for gentlemen that were not used to exercise. 'Hunting of the hare with greyhounds is a right good solace for men that be studious, of them to whom nature hath not given personage or courage apt for the wars,' wrote Sir Thomas Elyot in 1531. 'And also for gentlewomen, which fear neither sun nor wind for impairing their beauty. And peradventure they shall be threat less idle than they should be at home in their chambers.'

And for the onlookers, the contest between coursing dogs was determined not just by which caught the hare, but also by other performance points. There was, for instance, 'the cote', the moment when a greyhound, having overtaken the competing dog, turned the hare so that it ran in a different direction. Connoisseurs of the sport would watch closely for such moments.

Dover gave a prize, 'a silver-studded collar' for the winning greyhound. It is significant that the only two really costly prizes, the silver collar and the silver castle, were given in the events which attracted the gentry. Only rich men could be relied upon to hand back a valuable prize the following year for the next winner.

As well as equine sports, there were entertainments for the better-off onlookers. Dancing was an important part of the Olimpicks, and the dancers were probably local shepherds or villagers rather than the landowners. There is no mention of morris dancing at Dover's Games, perhaps because this traditional dance was associated with peasant church ales. In the morris dance sometimes a couple played

Robin Hood and Maid Marion, aided by a man dressed up as a hobby horse – sinful relics of paganism in Puritan eyes. Dover may have played safe by excluding morris dances.

Perhaps Dover organised rather more stylish dances than the rough and rural morris ones. 'Tripping nymphs do skip about the hills,' wrote one of the poets, and many of them refer to the beauty of the female dancers. The illustration of *Annalia Dubrensia* shows three women dancing without male partners. There is no illustration of morris dancers, traditionally all male with bells on their costumes, nor of the hobby horse. There is, however, a man playing what may be a bagpipe, a country instrument already out of place in sophisticated music circles. A contemporary manuscript says dismissively of the bagpipe, 'These pipes are never used by any artists in music; but by the more rustical sort of people.' So even if the women dancers are wearing ruffs and seem well dressed, it is likely that these are probably just the local village girls.

We know there was a 'dancing green' at the Games, and indeed the Olimpicks are at one point called a 'dancing assembly'. There is also mention of 'a matchless troop of female kind' so perhaps Dover encouraged a group of local girls to put on a dance display of some kind. He may even have rehearsed them and paid for costumes.

'Ancient dauncing Druids', which have been called on to the plain to dance a jig and then return into the woods, are mentioned by another poet. There *were* ancient barrows on Willersey Hill, not far from Kingcombe Plain, and it is just possible that Dover arranged for some dancers to dress up as Druids. But the reference may simply have been a bit of poetic fancy on the part of the writer, William Durham, the son of the local Willersey landowner.

There were also mixed dances. 'Youth intermixed with maids to memory bring the dancing of the ancient Druids,' wrote Dover's nephew – incidentally making another mention of dancing Druids! Another poet asks the attending maids to make up a coronet for Dover, while a third writes, 'Let a virgin, led with two lads, crown his head.' Perhaps there was a Queen of the May or Lady of the Games and a playful coronation using a wreath.

Homer, the ancient Greek poet, also put in an appearance. Perhaps he was a blind harper dressed up. Not only would a harper dressed as Homer have added entertainment to the hillside sports, he would also have made another link with the classical Olympic theme. William Denny, a friend of many years, recounts:

> While Homer's emblem on his harp did play
> Admired raptures, and sing many a lay,
> More full and sweet than all the choir of May.

In general the wandering musicians and minstrels of medieval times were out of fashion. Once, minstrels had been professional musicians of high status, either on the staff of the big houses or welcomed on a kind of progress between them. Now they were included among the rogues and sturdy beggars that the law punished, and later, under the Commonwealth of Oliver Cromwell after the Civil War, they would be prohibited altogether from playing even in inns or taverns.

'A poor fiddler ... is just so many strings above a beggar,' wrote John Earle. But despite this severe judgement the traditional blind harper or fiddler was still made welcome at country festivals and church ales in Dover's day. And Sir Philip Sidney, a generation earlier, had admitted his fondness for simple ballads of the past. 'Certainly I confess my own barbarousness: I never heard old song of Percy and Douglas [two ballad subjects], but my heart moved more than with a trumpet, yet is it sung by some blind crowder [fiddler], no rougher voice than rude style.'

Something of the old glamour still hung about a harper. The vicar who had entertained Queen Anne in Wiltshire with 'a pastoral' had thought it no shame to dress up as a bard among his parishioners. Antiquarian John Aubrey believed that the custom of keeping a minstrel went back to Trojan times. 'When I was a boy every gentleman almost kept a harper in his house; and some of them could versify. In Wales the gentlemen have their harpers ... and so have the Irish. 'Tis an old custom derived from the Trojans ...' If Dover also believed that a traditional harper was a link with ancient Troy, his blind Homer would have seemed a good idea for an occasion which made claims to an ancient Greek heritage.

Dover's other Trojan touch may have been a Troy town, one of the names given to a turf maze. Most mazes today are hedge mazes, where the paths are marked out by hedges which conceal the path from those treading the maze. The turf maze had a similar pattern, but in the place of the hedge was simply heaped-up turf. The small ridges might be only a foot high. Thus the maze path was hidden neither from onlookers nor from those following the path.

These were also known as Troy walls, Julian's bowers, shepherd's races, mizmazes and labyrinths (from the ancient Greek story of Theseus, killer of the Minotaur in its labyrinth). Villagers would often play some kind of dance or treading game, sometimes known as the Troy game, in the paths of the turf mazes. Dover would have been familiar with Plutarch's life of Theseus, in which the historian described the hero dancing 'a kind of dance, which the Delians keep to this day, as they say: in which there are many turns and returns, much after the turnings of the Labyrinth'.

The evidence in favour of a Troy town at the Olimpicks is twofold. First, several of the poets in *Annalia Dubrensia* refer to mazes or labyrinths even though they do not clearly say that one was part of the festival. Second, the frontispiece to *Annalia Dubrensia* shows a square device, looking rather like a knot garden pattern. Some researchers think this is

Dover's flag – 'a square plaque which I take to be a facsimile of Dover's yellow favour,' says one.

Although the pattern shows no maze path, I think the device is likely nonetheless to be a poor representation of a maze. Perhaps the artist misunderstood what a turf maze was and simply used a pattern he found in a gardening book. There are gardening books of the period which give patterns for knot gardens and mazes within the same cover. One well-known Elizabethan book, which ran to several editions, even had the title *The Gardener's Labyrinth,* which might have confused the illustrator.

The existence of Dover's maze is confirmed by John Aubrey, who took an interest in these mysterious turf ornaments. He wrote: 'Anciently (I believe) there were many of them in England: on the down between Blandford and Pimperne in Dorset, which was much used by the young people on holidays, and by the schoolboys. At West Ashton in Wilts, is another: and (I think) there is one on the Cotswold downs, where Mr Dover's Games were celebrated.' He added: 'I have reason to believe … that we received our use of Mazes (Labyrinths, Mizmazes) from the Danes … as they from the Egyptians and Greeks.'

Only a few turf mazes survive today and it is intriguing to

note that one of them remains in the private garden of a house not very far from Dover's Hill. It may have been the inspiration for Dover's maze or perhaps a copy of it. It is still well maintained and has given its name to the farm, Troy Farm.

Just like a blind harper dressed as Homer, a Troy town would have added to the ancient Greek theme of the Olimpicks. Though turf mazes probably originated from ecclesiastical sources (they are found in medieval French churches), Dover and his contemporaries believed them to be of classical origin. Like a blind harper dressed up as Homer, a Troy town would not have been too costly an entertainment. Although it might be trampled by the beasts grazing on the common later in the year, it could be restored to visibility with annual re-cutting by Dover's gardener.

The other entertainments at the Olimpicks were booths or tents for card games. This was probably an innovation by Dover since the particular card games he laid on were not among the usual activities of church ales. Such games had the approval of King James, who had written in *Basilicon Doron*:

I will not therefore agree with the curiosity of some learned men in our age, in forbidding cards, dice and

other such like games of hazard ... Not that thereby I take the defence of vain carders and dicers, that waste their moyen and their time (whereof few consider the preciousness) upon prodigal and continual playing ... But only I cannot condemn you at some times, when you have no other thing ado (as a good King will be seldom) and are weary of reading, or evil disposed in your person, and when it is foul and stormy weather; then, I say, may ye lawfully play at cards or tables.

It seems likely that the card games at the Olimpicks may have been played for low stakes. William Basse, one of the celebratory poets, says specifically that nobody leaves the hillside having lost too much money:

> Where none, a little gold so spent,
> Nor time, more precious, need repent.
> Where no vain card, nor witching dy [dice]
> Doth gamester strip of lands or clothes.

And it is from another poet, William Denny, that we know exactly what card games were played:

> In Cotswold tents are sports of all conditions;
> The studious game of chess for politicians
> To hammer plots; and Irish for probation
> Of each man's virtue, how to master passion;
> Cent for those gentry who their states have marred;
> That game befits them, for they must discard.

King James did not particularly approve of chess, on the grounds it was too obsessive a game.

> I think it over fond, because it is over wise and
> philosophic a folly; for where all such light plays

are ordained to free men's heads for a time, from the fashious thoughts on their affairs, it by the contrary filleth and troubleth men's heads, with as many fashious toys of the play, as before it was filled with thoughts on his affairs.

Robert Burton, on the other hand, thought the obsessive nature of chess was an advantage in driving out other thoughts. It was 'a good and witty exercise of the mind for some kind of men, and fit for such melancholy … as are idle, and have extravagant impertinent thoughts, or troubled with cares, nothing better to distract their mind and alter their meditations'.

Irish, a game like backgammon and one of the two other games mentioned, was another taxing game. 'Irish is an ingenious game, and requires a great deal of skill to play it well, especially the after-game. It is not to be learned otherwise than by observation and practice,' wrote Charles Cotton in *The Compleat Gamester* of 1674. The so-called after-game depended partly on dice and was so complicated that Cotton admitted, 'I know not what instructions to give you, you must herein trust to your own judgement and the chance of the dice, and if they run low for some time it will be so much the better.' Apparently one unlucky throw of the dice could ruin the most skilful game.

Cent, a game like picquet, was so called because, as its name suggests, the scoring system centred round the score of one hundred. The game was also known as Mount Saint and required two players, each with a pack but minus all the cards below seven. As it is not mentioned in *The Compleat Gamester* it was probably not a very fashionable game by the second half of the century. A list of card games from 1629 gives some idea of the card games passed over by Dover. Judging by names alone, some of these do not belong in high society circles – 'ruff, trump, slam'e, gleek, newcut, swig, loadam, putt, primifisty, post and pair, bone-ace, anakin, seven cards, one and thirty, my sow has pigged'.

Reviewing the entertainments and sports that Dover arranged for his social equals or superiors, it is clear that he was careful in his choice of amusements. He distinguished his Olimpicks from coarse rural amusements by the addition of classical amusements such as a blind Homer and a turf Troy town. And almost everything we read in the poems about the Games suggests that he was also trying to avoid controversy.

AN ECLOGUE ON THE PALLIA AND NOBLE ASSEMBLIES REVIVED ON COTSWOLD HILLS BY *MR ROBERT DOVER*

Some melancholy swains about have gone
To teach all zeal their own complexion;
Choler they will admit sometimes, I see
But phlegm and sanguine no religions be.
These teach that dancing is a Jezebel
And barley break the ready way to hell;
The morris, idols; Whitsun ales can be
But the profane relics of a Jubilee.
These in a zeal, t'express how much they do
The organs hate, have silenced bagpipes too;
And harmless maypoles, all are railed upon,
As if they were the towers of Babylon ...

The country lass, although her dance be good,
Stirs not another's galliard in the blood;
And yet their sports by some controlled have been,
Who think there is no mirth but what is sin.
Oh, might I but their harmless gambols see
Restored unto an ancient liberty.

THOMAS RANDOLPH

Chapter 5

THE FIRST
Olimpick Controversy

When Robert Dover rode out at Whitsun to open his Olimpick Games, he was wearing King James I's second-hand clothes. We don't know exactly what these were but we know that they included a hat with a feather in it and a ruff from the royal wardrobe. These were the outward and visible signs of royal approval. They were also the visible signs of the controversy that was to surround these Olimpicks.

There had been controversial Olympic Games before, even in ancient Olympia. Although in theory the Sacred Truce during the games should have ensured neutrality, there was always the threat of invasion from the Spartans, who had been banned from the games. The modern games have had their controversies too. The USA boycotted the Moscow Olympics on the grounds (there is an irony now) of the USSR's invasion of Afghanistan. Then the Russians in turn boycotted the Los Angeles Olympics, sometimes known as the 'private enterprise games', in a tit-for-tat move.

The controversy surrounding the first ever British Olimpicks was about sin and politics. In the seventeenth-century world, religious enthusiasts believed that even the smallest action might lead to sin, and sin (without repent-

ance and penance) would lead straight to hell. Even a small sin, a sin as light as a feather, could end up with you burning in hell after your death for all eternity.

So wearing a hat with a jaunty feather at the time of the first Olimpicks was not just a fashion statement. It was a party political and religious statement too. It put Robert Dover firmly in the camp of those that were not Puritans. Puritans wore hats, but they certainly didn't wear hats with feathers. A generation earlier Puritan writer Philip Stubbes had ranted against rich hats of all kinds.

> Some are of silk, some of velvet, some of taffeta, some of sarcenet, some of wool, and which is more curious, some of a certain kind of fine hair: these they call beaver hats of twenty, thirty or forty shillings a piece, fetched from beyond the seas, from whence a great sort of other vanities do come besides.

We don't know what material made up Robert Dover's royal hat, but we know it included a feather. 'And another sort (as fantastical as the rest),' complained Philip Stubbes in his *The Anatomy of Abuses*, a bestselling Puritan book, 'are content with no kind of hat, without a great plume of feathers of divers and sundry colours, peaking on top of their heads, not unlike (I dare not say) cockscombs, but fool's baubles if you list.'

In Puritan eyes, feathers were 'flags of defiance to virtue'. They led to sin. 'These feathers argue the lightness of their fond imaginations and plainly convince them of instability and folly, for sure I am, handsome they cannot be. Therefore ensigns of pride they must needs be.'

Ruffs were no better. In the generation before Robert Dover, ruffs had been up to a quarter of a yard (nearly 250mm) out from the neck. Jacobean ruffs stuck out less, but since we know that Robert Dover had a ruff that had belonged to a king, we can assume it was a fine one – and probably starched! Puritans like Philip Stubbes felt that the devil was in the starch. 'A certain kind of liquid matter, which they call starch, wherein the Devil hath learned them to wash and die their ruffs, which being dry, will then stand stiff and inflexible about their necks.'

It might seem odd to us that trivia such as the exact

material on a hat or the presence of starch in linen should cause controversy. But there was worse in Puritan eyes. The very idea of games to celebrate a church holiday such as Whitsun brought out the most rabid disapproval from the religious party.

We need to remember that there was no idea of the secular state and few people believed in the ideal of religious toleration. The religion of the country was the religion of its monarch and had swung from Protestant Edward VI to Catholic Mary, then back again to Protestant Elizabeth.

The idea that a person's religion was their own private business was simply not acceptable. All sides worked towards the triumph of their religious point of view – and if blood had to be shed, so be it.

King James was the Protestant candidate for the English throne and his succession, after the death of Elizabeth I, owed as much to his religion as to his blood tie. He himself had been brought up in the fierce Scottish kirk and Protestantism had been whipped into him by his Puritan tutor. Other young kings before him, like Edward VI, had had a whipping boy, a boy who took physical punishment on behalf of the royal body, but George Buchanan, James' tutor, used to box the infant king's ears. Even Buchanan's contemporaries might have considered this insufficiently deferential.

James' first intense same-sex relationship (and there were to be several of these in his life) was with a Catholic, his French cousin Esme Stuart, Sieur d'Aubigny. In the country as a whole after Guy Fawkes' gunpowder plot, which threatened to blow up both king and Parliament, the fear of Catholicism was widespread. But James was almost as severe on Puritans as on Catholics. In a speech to Parliament he outlined the three different beliefs that he had found in his new realm.

> The first is the true religion, which by me is pro-
> fessed, and by the law is established: the second is
> the falsely called Catholics, but truly papists; the
> third (which I called a sect rather than religion), is
> the Puritans ... who do not so far differ from us in
> points of religion, as in their confused form of policy
> and parity, being ever discontented with the present
> government, and impatient to suffer any superiority,
> which maketh their sect unable to be suffered in any
> well-governed Commonwealth.

What he saw in Puritanism – correctly, as it was to turn out – was a challenge to monarchical authority.

And emotionally, if not officially, the king was often on the Catholic or at least the Anglo-Catholic side. The anti-Puritan party, a loose collection of traditional and what we would now call Anglo-Catholic Church of England believers, were more inclined to support his cherished belief in the divine right of kings. The king also had more in common with them than the Puritans when it came to recreations. Sports were going to be a battlefield between the two sides, one of the several theoretical battlefields that would eventually lead to real warfare, the Civil War between Monarchists and Parliamentarians.

When King James first came to the English throne, it seemed that he was of the Puritan point of view about sports. He had responded graciously, though without committing himself, to a Puritan petition asking for more reforms. In the early years of his reign he had drawn up articles for Ireland in which he had forbidden anything other than religious exercises on a Sunday. It was, after all, the Lord's day. But (as we might forget nowadays) Sunday was also the only day off for working people, who worked long hours. So for many people Sunday was the only possible day for organised sports. Even so Puritans disapproved.

'I know these sports have many oppugners, whole volumes writ against them ... Some out of preposterous zeal object many times trivial arguments, and because of some abuse will quite take away the good use, as if they should forbid wine because it makes men drunk; but in my judgement they are too stern,' wrote Robert Burton in his *Anatomy of*

Melancholy published in 1621. 'I … was ever of that mind, those May games, wakes and Whitsun ales, etc., if they be not at unseasonable hours, may justly be permitted. Let them freely feast, sing and dance, have their puppet plays, hobby horses, tabors, crowds, bagpipes, etc., play at ball, and barley breaks, and what sports and recreations they like best.'

The upper classes had always had plenty of chance to enjoy themselves. Dancing and music were a part, not just of court life, but also of the life of big country landowners. Manly sports were part of a gentleman's education and country sports like hunting and coursing were practised by most of those who could afford to do so.

King James, in his book *Basilicon Doron*, had declared: 'Certainly bodily exercises and games are very commendable, as well for banishing of idleness, the mother of all vice; as for making the body able and durable for travel, which is very necessary for a king.'

However, what was all right for the master might nevertheless not be suitable for the manservant. A certain fear had always surrounded the amusements of the lower orders. A Puritan preacher as early as 1579 had lamented the fact

that the laws against sturdy beggars were not put into effect. If they had been, there would not be so many 'loitering persons, so many ruffians, blasphemers, swing bucklers, so many drunkards, tosspots, whoremasters, dancers, fiddlers and minstrels, dice players, maskers, fencers, thieves, interlude players [i.e. actors], cutpurses, cousiners [cheats], masterless servants, jugglers, rogues, sturdy beggars, counterfeit Egyptians …'

The authorities were always worried that popular festivals might get out of control.

Church or parish wakes, revels, May games, plays
and such other unlawful assemblies of the people

of sundry parishes into one parish on the Sabbath Day and other times, is a special cause that many disorders, contempts of law, and other enormities are there perpetrated and committed, to the great profanation of the Lord's Sabbath, the dishonour of Almighty God, increase of bastardy and of dissolute life, and of many other mischiefs and inconveniences ...

an order of justices had declared eight years before James' accession. So while games on the holy Sabbath were a spiritual issue, games on any day of the week might become a law-and-order issue if they gave rise to disorderly behaviour.

King James, however, did not swerve from his opinion (held before ever he arrived in England) that the common people would be more contented if they were allowed some festivities. About five years after the probable starting date of Dover's Olimpicks, he decided to reiterate his views. He had paid his first visit to Scotland since he had left to take up the English crown, and was returning to London. The visit had been notable for the trouble between him and the Puritan Scottish kirk, but James had enjoyed himself hunting almost every day on the journey back. He had travelled with musicians and in the evenings there had been music and dancing.

Then in Lancashire, on his way back to London, he had received a petition from 'some servants, labourers, mechanics and other vulgar persons complaining that they were debarred from dancing, playing, church ales – in a word, from all recreations on a Sunday after divine service'. James promptly granted them a licence for their activities. Lancashire was a county known for its religious backwardness. It included a large number of Catholics. There was also a vigorous Puritan party, which had been attempting to stop Sunday games altogether. The king, as he explained later, felt that this was a bar to the conversion of Catholics, who would feel that the Church of England was against 'honest mirth or recreation'.

Naturally the Lancashire decision had not gone down well with the Puritans. Nevertheless the king stuck to his guns. A year later, in 1618, he brought out *The King's Majesty's Declaration Concerning Lawful Sports*. This has always been known as *The King's Book of Sports* though it is a declaration, not a book. Its aim was to clarify his Lancashire decision and extend it to the rest of England.

King James explained:

> Whereas we did justly in our progress through Lancashire, rebuke some Puritans and precise people … in the prohibiting and unlawful punishing of our good people for using their lawful recreations, and honest exercises, after the afternoon sermon or service, we now find that two sorts of people wherewith that country is much infected (we mean papists and Puritans), have maliciously traduced and calumniated those our just and honourable proceedings.

King James argued that sports were good for the common people because it made 'their bodies more able for war, when we or our successors, shall have occasion to use them'. He maintained, as we often do, that people needed recreation on their days off, and if they were busy exercising they were keeping out of the pub and out of trouble. A ban on sports and games 'sets up filthy tipplings and drunkenness, and breeds a number of idle and discontented speeches in their ale houses. For when shall the common people have leave to exercise, if not upon the Sundays and holy days seeing they must apply their labour, and win their living in all working days?'

He was anxious to specify sports that appealed to respectable people, and to leave out the controversial sports that might be associated with hooligan behaviour. These were bear baiting, bull baiting and plays (sometimes called interludes). 'But withal we do here account still as prohibited all unlawful games to be used upon Sundays only, as bear and bull baitings, interludes, and at all times, in the meaner sort of people, by law prohibited, bowling.' These sports could be enjoyed by the gentry, who did not work on the other six days a week, but were prohibited to the working people, who did. Then as now, the authorities worried more about the moral welfare of the people below them rather than the moral welfare of their own section of society.

The king also much disliked football ('meeter for laming

than making able the users thereof') but did not specifically ban it. Only bowling was prohibited 'at all times' to the common people. Nowadays bowling on grass lawns is a pastime of the elderly rather than the young, and even ten-pin bowling is hardly associated with vice. But in the seventeenth century bowling had a reputation for gambling, drinking and cheating. The Cavalier fast set was to be found gambling on the bowling greens.

An example of the moral turpitude encouraged by bowling was Sir John Suckling. According to John Aubrey, he was

> the greatest gamester, both for bowling and cards, so that no shopkeeper would trust him for 6d, as today, for instance, he might by winning, be worth 200 pounds, and the next day he might not be worth half so much, or perhaps sometimes be *minus nihilo*. He was one of the best bowlers of his time in England. He played at cards rarely well and did use to practise by himself a-bed, and there studied how the best way of managing the cards could be. His sisters would come to the Peccadillo bowling green, crying for fear he should loose all their portions.

Various attempts to ban bowling had been made in the previous two centuries. 'Common bowling alleys ... eat up the credit of many idle citizens, whose gains at home are not able to weight down their losses abroad,' wrote another Puritan writer. So the king's prohibition of bowling, odd though it may seem to us, was a necessary part of making sure that Sabbath games included only respectable sports!

What was allowed in King James' *Book of Sports* was

> any lawful recreation, such as dancing, either of men or women, archery for men, leaping, vaulting, or any other such harmless recreation, nor from the having of May games, Whitsun ales, and morris dances, and the setting up of maypoles, and other sports therewith used, so as the same be had in due and convenient time, without impediment or neglect of divine service.

By specifying that these sports, including the much-hated (by the Puritans) maypoles, were allowable, the king had ranged himself with the party opposing the would-be religious reformers.

The rift between Puritans and Cavaliers could only widen. Philip Stubbes had already condemned the way some people kept the Sabbath: 'in May games, church ales, feasts and wakes: in piping, dancing, dicing, carding, bowling, tennis playing: in bear baiting, cockfighting, hawking, hunting and such like. In keeping of fairs and markets on the Sabbath. In football playing, and such other devilish pastimes.' His ideal, and the ideal of most Puritans, was a Sunday spent not in 'vain exercises, as please ourselves, but in such godly exercises as he in his holy word hath commanded', such as prayer, praise and reading religious books.

Puritans particularly disliked the rural dancing that took place on such country occasions, whether during a church ale or the Cotswold Olimpicks. Even though dancing was mentioned several times in the Bible, even though David had danced in front of the Lord, they were suspicious of almost all dancing. 'Dancing is the vilest vice of all, and truly it cannot easily be said what mischiefs the sight and the hearing do receive hereby, which afterward be the causes of communication and embracing,' wrote a minister in 1579. 'Maidens and matrons are groped and handled with unchaste hands, and kissed and dishonestly embraced: the things, which nature hath hidden, and modesty covered, are then often times by means of lasciviousness made naked, and ribaldry under the colour of pastime is dissembled, an exercise doubtless not descended from heaven, but by the devils of hell devised.'

The Anatomy of Abuses, in a section titled 'The Horrible Vice of Pestiferous Dancing in England', even claimed that dancing was bad for the physique. 'I have known divers [i.e. various people], that by the immoderate use thereof, have in a short time become decrepit and lame, so remaining to their dying day. Some have broken their legs with skipping, leaping, turning and vaulting ...' Worse still was the effect of immoderate dance on the mind – 'never any came from it without some part of his mind broken and lame, such a wholesome exercise it is'.

Stubbes too argued that dancing produced lust. 'All lewd, wanton and lascivious dancing in public assemblies and conventicles without respect, either of sex, kind, time, place, person, or anything else, by the warrant of the word of God, I do utterly condemn.' There were 'beastly slabberings, kissings, and smoochings, with other filthy gestures.' He wondered if single-sex dancing in a private home, used in the fear of the Lord, might be acceptable, but not the kind of thing that Robert Dover was encouraging up on the hill above Weston sub Edge. That sort of dancing would only end up in sin and spiritual harm.

(On one issue at least Stubbes was in line with modern thinking. In a passage of striking modernity, he complained of bear baiting, 'What Christian heart can take pleasure to see one poor beast to rend, tear and kill another, and all for his foolish pleasure? ... And shall we abuse the creatures of God, yea, take pleasure in abusing them, and yet think that the contumely done to them, redoundeth not to him who made them?')

Sermons, treatises and books thundered out, with both sides quoting from the Bible to make their point. Today's historians call these Puritan books 'complaint literature'. Complaint literature started in Elizabethan England, fell back somewhat, then redoubled in vigour in the reign of Charles I.

Some authors went further than Philip Stubbes. It wasn't just that you might break a leg by leaping, vaulting or dancing in these unsuitable Sunday sports and Whitsun ales. God himself might strike you dead. In 1636, eleven years after James' death, there was a book published with the splendidly long title of *A Divine Tragedy Lately Acted, Or A Collection of sundry memorable examples of God's judgement on Sabbath-breakers, and other like Libertines, in their unlawful sports, happening within the Realm of England, in the compass only of two years last past, since the Book was published, worthy to be known and considered of all men, especially such, who are guilty of the same or Arch-patrons thereof.*

Like Stubbes before him, the anonymous author was mainly concerned with the profanation of the Sabbath which should be 'wholly, only, and entirely ... spent in religious public and private duties of God's worship and that dancing, sports, and pastimes, on it, are sinful and execrable'. But he mentioned, with approval, a cleric who had condemned 'dancing, mummeries, masks, and such like Bacchanals (which he simply condemns at all times, but especially on sacred festivals and the Lord's days as most detestable profanations of them)'. So even though Dover's Olimpicks were held not on the Sabbath but on weekdays, they would fall into the category of being sinful.

Did the writer, usually identified as a Puritan clergyman called Henry Burton, know about Robert Dover's Olimpicks? We don't know for sure. But Burton had probably drawn on a network of Puritan vicars sending in awful cases of divine retribution from their localities, and the very first example came from Gloucestershire, Dover's own county. 'A miller at Churchdown, near Gloucester, would needs (contrary to the admonitions both of his minister in private, and generally in public, yea and that very day, or of other Christian friends), keep a solemn Whitsun ale.' It was as bad as it could be. The miller had put musical instruments near the church ready, stored provisions in the church itself, and after the sermon everybody fell to dancing. The miller returnéd to his house with the revellers and 'about 9 of the clock on Whitsunday, a fire took suddenly in the house over their heads and was so brief and quick, that it burnt down his house and mill, and devoured all with the greatest of all his other provision and household stuff.'

Another example of God's judgement on sinners occurred in the same county. 'One in Gloucestershire being very forward to advance a solemn summer meeting wherein his son was to be a cheese sticker, went himself in great jollity to see it, and there beholding it, he fell down suddenly and so died.' If God could strike you down just for going to the local church ale, then clearly these country entertainments were evil occasions.

The court party, of course, were on the side first of King James and then of his son and successor, King Charles I. They too produced sermons, poetry and books. Some of the poems in *Annalia Dubrensia* tried to answer the complaint literature. One book, with a title as long if not longer than any written by Puritans, was published during the reign of Charles I: *The Communion Book Catechism Expounded, According to God's holy Word, and the established Doctrine of the*

Church. Written for the furtherance of youth and ignorant persons, in the understanding of the grounds and principles of the true Christian Religion, set forth by public authority. Wherein also are explained sundry of the highest points in Divinity, and matters greatly considerable in these present times. In special there is demonstrated, that His most excellent Majesty's Declaration to his Subjects, concerning lawful sports to be used, doth tend unto a very great increase of true godliness through the whole Kingdom.

This followed the royal line that Sunday sports were necessary for good health, pointing out that many servants worked hard for six days a week, then were expected by their employers to attend both morning and evening service 'and if they may not after evening service walk abroad and take the air, and refresh their spirits, how is it possible that they can long continue in health? How much is the life of such servants, different from the life of slaves among the Turks?'

The author, Edmund Reeve, had harsh and pungent words for the Puritans.

There is a generation which will strain at gnats and swallow up camels: which will take offence at their honest poor neighbour recreating himself in the Sunday evening, and they themselves keep in their own houses, swelling with spiritual pride, vain glory and hypocrisy, envy, hatred, and malice, and all uncharitableness, blood thirstiness and rejoicing in others' calamities, and given unto unexpressable lying and circumventing, and uncivility.

The Whitsun games and wakes were authorised by God.

Moreover in keeping of the wakes, our forefathers not only expressed every year a grateful remembrance and thanksgiving unto God for their churches builded, but also would unto that their said feast invite their friends of the parishes round about or

near them, and then when their neighbours' wakes were, they were invited again. Thus the whole land feasted each other unto an unutterable conservation [*sic*] of unity and godly love ... When as dancing was often used in all the parishes by all people, how greatly was true Christian friendship increased thereby, and conserved.

The sports controversy was reflected not just in but also by the judiciary. On King Charles' accession to the throne, in need of a grant from Parliament the new king reluctantly consented to an Act 'for punishing divers abuses committed on the Lord's Day, called Sunday'. This forbade bear baiting, bull baiting, interludes, plays 'or other unlawful exercises and pastimes' within the parish, and also forbade any meetings of people outside their own parishes on Sundays. Puritan landowners had already begun to forbid their servants and farm workers to attend church ales or Sunday sports.

Then in 1632 two judges on circuit in Somerset went further and took it upon themselves to order that

> in regard of the infinite number of inconveniences daily arising by means of revels; that such revels, church ales, clerk ales, and all other public ales be henceforth utterly suppressed ... and for the avoiding the concourse of idle people it is further ordered, that minstrels and such others persons as usually carry up and down bulls and bears to bait ... shall be punished as rogues.

This judicial order, which went further than the previous act on Sunday abuses, was reversed by the king, and a year later Charles I republished the *Book of Sports.*

> We find that under pretence of taking away abuses, there hath been a general forbidding, not only of ordinary meetings, but of the feast of the dedication of the churches, commonly called wakes. Now our express will and pleasure is, that these feasts, with others, shall be observed, and that our Justices of the

Peace, in their several divisions, shall look to it, both
that all disorders there may be prevented or punished,
and that all neighbourhood and freedom, with man-
like and lawful exercises be used.

The battle became fiercer when King Charles ordered that
the republished *Book of Sports* should be read in all churches.
Ministers who refused to do so were prosecuted. Others con-
formed reluctantly. Thus a controversy about sport contributed
to the growing ill-feeling between king and Puritans.

By keeping control of his Games and preventing drunkenness and disorder, Robert Dover could satisfy those who
objected to the bad behaviour at such occasions. But even
when he managed the crowds and directed only lawful sports,
he could not satisfy those Puritans who considered the activities themselves either innately sinful or an occasion for sin.

He had put himself firmly in the king's camp by continuing to hold his annual Olimpick Games, by allowing dancing
and music on the hillside, and even by wearing the jaunty
feather in his hat – that flag of 'defiance to virtue'. The future
of his Games, the first Olimpicks, would depend on which
side won the bloody contest that was about to start.

TO

Mr Robert Dover,

UPON HIS ANNUAL SPORTS

AT COTSWOLD

Hear! You bad owners of enclosèd grounds,
That have your souls as narrow as your bounds!
When you have robbed the earth of her increase,
Stored up that fading treasure, and spoke peace
Unto your wretched thoughts, the barren field
Of Cotswold, and those emulous hills shall yield
A crop of honour unto Dover's name,
Richer than all your stacks or barns contain!
Shepherds, rejoice! 'Tis he shall make you free,
And every year proclaim a jubilee!
He shall invite there many a lusty swain,
To strive in hope of glory and of gain!
Pan, for his sake, shall often pass that way,
And make your mountains his Arcadia.

SHACKERLEY MARMION

Chapter 6

THE END
AND THE
RESTORATION
OF THE
First Olimpicks

It was June 1644 and the king's forces were on the move. 'From Broadway, the King and all his army marched over the Cotswold Downs, where Dover's games were, to Stow in the Wold six mile,' wrote Richard Symond, who kept a diary of the Royalist army movements with notes on interesting monuments in the towns and villages he passed. King Charles and his Cavaliers were on their way first to Burford, then Witney, where he was joined by 'pike and colours, for before there was none marched with the King this march'.

The king had raised his standard at Nottingham two years earlier and his army, based at Oxford, had won several battles but failed to take London. The Cotswolds, like other parts of the country, had become a field of war criss-crossed by armies of both the king and the Parliament. Gloucestershire was divided between the country upland areas, which usually supported the king, and the valley towns that, with Chipping Campden as the exception to the rule, usually supported Parliament. The cathedral town of Gloucester, in particular, stood firm against the king.

In the country as a whole, the Civil War cost the lives of 80,000 people who fell in battle and a further 100,000 or so who were killed in accidents or by disease. Many of those at the Dover Olimpicks, the onlooking gentry, the local shepherds engaged in wrestling or cudgel play and the girls who danced on the hillside, were to suffer loss of either life or goods. Villages were looted by armies on the march; towns were besieged and overrun. Friendly armies were just as devastating as enemy forces, usually stealing whatever a place possessed.

An Oxfordshire villager made an inventory of what he had lost to Parliamentary soldiers – seven pairs of sheets, three brass kettles, two brass pots, five pewter dishes, four shirts, four smocks, two coats, one clock, one waistcoat, seven dozen candles, a frying pan, a spit, two pairs of pot hooks, one peck of wheat, four bags, some oatmeal, some salt, a basketful of eggs, bowls, dishes, spoons, ladles, drinking pots and 'whatsoever else they could lay their hands on'.

At the other end of the social scale a landowner near Stow-on-the-Wold, not far from Dover's Hill, paid out nearly £447, detailed in fifty-six entries in his accounts, in spoiled crops, stolen cattle, bribes to soldiers to go away and the cost of quartering others. At the same time his yearly income from fairs in the town fell from £77 a year before the war to nothing in 1644, when plague hit the town, and only £5 10s 7d the following year. A huge loss of income.

Royalist soldiers behaved no better than Parliamentarian

ones. In Chipping Campden, the commander of its Cavalier garrison, Sir Henry Bard, put out a proclamation to the countryside warning 'unless you bring unto me ... the monthly contribution for six months, you are to expect an unsanctified troop of horse among you from whom, if you hide yourselves, they shall fire your house without mercy, hang up your bodies wherever they find them, and scare your ghosts.'

The Olimpicks had ceased by the time the king marched across Dover's Hill. Perhaps a new Puritan vicar of nearby Chipping Campden had something to do with their end. Wakes and sports had no place in the Puritan world, and in London the Puritans were to pull down the beautiful cross in Cheapside and order the hangman to ceremonially burn *The Book of Sports* on its site in 1643. It is more likely, however, that the Games stopped because war broke out and Kingcombe Plain, soon to be known as Dover's Hill, was in the path of armies. At a time of real artillery, there was no place for a summer castle with blank cannon fire. Those who thought sport would bring peace between people had been confounded.

Atrocities were committed by both sides. Surrendering

soldiers were sometimes killed nonetheless. John Aubrey, in his *Natural History of Wiltshire*, writes of one such incident: 'On this oak, Sir Francis Dodington hung up thirteen [soldiers] after quarter [i.e. after they had surrendered]. He made a son hang his father or *e contra*.' It is on record that when the Royalists took Cirencester, they locked 1,100 prisoners in the church for two days without food or water, then marched them to Oxford in the snow even though some were without coats, doublets, shoes or even breeches. At Oxford, 'his Majesty, with the Prince [Rupert] and the Duke of York, came thither to see us drove along more like dogs and horses than men, up to the knees in mire and dirt'.

Two years after the king's army had marched across Dover's Hill towards Stow-on-the-Wold, the hillside was the scene of one of the last battles of the Civil War. In March 1646 Colonel Birch of the Parliamentary army was deployed on the high ground, looking down into the valley where Sir Jacob Astley, a Royalist commander, was marching 3,000 men from Worcestershire towards Oxford where he hoped to join the king. Birch decided to harass his rearguard, as the remnant of the king's army toiled up the hill towards Stow-on-the-Wold.

Just before Stow-on-the-Wold the Parliamentarians attacked. Astley's force was overwhelmed and defeated. The grey-haired Cavalier general sat down wearily on a drum in the middle of his captors. 'You have done your work, boys, and may go play, unless you will fall out among yourselves,' he said. The Cavaliers had lost the war.

In the struggle between king and Parliament, Robert Dover was, like Sir Jacob Astley, on the losing side, loyal to the king. Nicholas Wallington, a clerical contributor to *Annalia Dubrensia*, had made Dover's allegiance explicit when he wrote about the amazing social harmony of the Olimpicks:

> Dover, strange monarchs and their force despiseth;
> He bows to none, his Charles he only prizeth;
> He is invincible to all but one;
> To's King he yields, or else he yields to none! …
> Who durst assemble such a troop as he,
> But might of insurrection charged be?
> His soldiers, though they every one dissent

In minds and manners, yet his merriment
Ones them; lords, knights, swains, shepherds,
   churls agree
To crown his sports: discords make harmony.

Like others before him, Wallington felt that sport had a cohesive effect on society, bringing together those of high and humble estate. It was then, and perhaps is now, mere wishful thinking, held mainly by those in the upper reaches of society. For the Civil War split not just the country, but those who had attended the Games.

Most of Dover's friends and relations joined the king's party and suffered for the cause when Parliament won. But at least four of the poets were in their graves before war broke out. Michael Drayton died five years before *Annalia Dubrensia* was published, and Thomas Randolph a year before. Ben Jonson died a year after and Shackerley Marmion two years later. Marmion had joined Sir John Suckling's troop of horse, a body of men who dressed in white doublets, scarlet coats and feathers in their hats. He fell ill during a campaign against the Scots, was taken back to London and died in 1639, before the beginning of the Civil War.

Dover himself may have joined the king's army and followed his monarch over the hill where his Games had been held. He was described as 'Captain' Dover in 1691. But it is more likely this title is a confusion between father and son. His son John Dover became a captain of horse under Prince Rupert, the dashing prince whose cavalry charges devastated the Parliamentary army in the first stages of the war. The Dover family may even have met the Prince, since there was a tradition that Rupert visited the Dover Olimpicks with Endymion Porter.

Robert Dover, aged sixty by the time King Charles raised his standard, probably stayed at home during the war. He was to live long enough to see his side lose the war, to hear of the execution of the king who had supported his Games, and the advent of a republican Commonwealth. He died in Barton-on-the-Heath, probably at his son's house, aged seventy, the year before Oliver Cromwell was made Protector.

His son, the cavalry officer, retired to the country and, like other Royalists who did not take part in public life, lived to see the restoration of the monarchy.

Robert Dover's friend and patron, Endymion Porter, stayed close to his king during the war. He became, at the age of fifty-five, the colonel of a foot regiment, but took little part in the fighting. He acted more like a staff officer to the king at all times, rather than as the commander of a regiment. He narrowly escaped being captured at the Battle of Edgehill when Rupert's cavalry charged off into the distance leaving the king and his companions unprotected.

Endymion's son, George Porter, had also joined the army and became the drinking companion of Lord Goring, the Royalist general. Goring described George as 'the best company but worst officer that ever served the king'. George Porter's drunkenness and slowness to obey orders contributed to more than one military setback. He was taken prisoner, but despite his poor reputation was swapped for a Parliamentary officer. His father had the shame of seeing him desert to the Parliamentary side in 1645.

Endymion himself was ordered to carry letters from the king to the queen in Paris. But he was not welcome there. 'Here in our court no man looks on me,' he wrote sadly, 'and the queen thinks I lost my estates from want of wit rather than from my loyalty to my master.' Then, in the year that his monarch was tried and executed, he too returned to Britain from penniless exile and compounded with Parliament.

He claimed that though he had attended the king throughout, he 'never took upon him any commands or did bear arms in the said war'.

He had suffered already. An inventory of his possessions shows that he had lent £10,000, a fortune in those days, to the late king and that all his pictures and valuables from his London house had been seized by the Parliamentary authorities. He died later that year. His turncoat son, who paid the fine imposed by the authorities on his father, lived to become a favourite at the court of Charles II.

Among the poets of *Annalia Dubrensia* William Denny was imprisoned for Royalist plotting and on release lived in great poverty during the Commonwealth. Sir John Mennes fought for his king and shared the poverty-stricken exile of Charles II. He lived long enough to be made an admiral after the restoration of the monarchy, joining Samuel Pepys at the Navy Board. (Pepys thought the aged cavalier an 'old fool' and had to do most of his work for him.)

John Monson, a lawyer who contributed to *Annalia Dubrensia*, declared for the king and then, when the Royalist cause failed, was put in charge of the negotiations for the surrender of Oxford, previously the royal headquarters. Monson suffered for his loyalty but was permitted a quiet retirement.

Sir William Davenant, a friend of Endymion Porter's, whose poem found its way into the later edition of the *Annalia Dubrensia*, also fought for the king and was knighted at the Siege of Gloucester. In 1650 he spent two years in prison. One story is that he was only saved from execution when one of the Parliamentarians, Harry Marten, joked: 'In sacrifices they always offered pure and without blemish; now ye talk of making a sacrifice of an old rotten rascal.' Davenant lived to see the restoration of the monarchy. (Lord Falkland used the same jest to save the regicide Marten from execution though not from prison.)

It was difficult to stay neutral. One of the poets, however, William Ambrose, seems to have kept his head down, managing to get on with life despite the difficulties of living in a county with two armies on the march. Throughout the war Ambrose kept his two positions as headmaster of Evesham Grammar School and vicar of a living nearby, and even stayed in post during the Commonwealth for a few years.

Nor were all Dover's friends on the king's side. William Durham, son of a landowner only two miles from Dover's Hill, came out for Parliament. When war broke out, he became chaplain to the Speaker of the House of Commons. He had written one of the longer poems in praise of the Games, probably when he was in his early twenties. Perhaps he joined the Parliamentarians for political not religious reasons.

Possibly he had a change of heart and was converted to Puritanism. Later on, he turned from writing poetry to publishing sermons and tracts. Or perhaps he just saw where his best interests lay. Not all people who supported country games supported the king, just as not all people who disliked country games supported Parliament. Durham flourished under the Commonwealth, but his turn to suffer came at the restoration of the monarchy. He was ejected from his rich living.

Fun and games were in short supply under the victorious Commonwealth. All the saints' days had been abolished by Parliament. Christmas feasting and the traditional decorations of holly and ivy were banned, and in London soldiers would even enter private houses to stop any celebration or religious observance. A fine of £5 was enacted against the publication of any book that encouraged sports on the Sabbath. Even the wretched and tortured bears of the Hope Theatre in London were shot to put an end to bear baiting. The stumps of broken wayside crosses in Cotswold villages today are testament to Puritan wreckers in the countryside.

Dover's Olimpicks might be ended, but the idea of games was not forgotten among the exiled Cavaliers. The Duke of Newcastle presented the future Charles II with a treatise on government 'for your Majesty when you are enthroned'. (He assured Charles that there was nothing in his treatise 'stolen out of books, for I seldom or ever read any'.) The duke, a bit of a compulsive writer, believed, as earlier royal supporters had, that the common people needed amusements. He recommended bringing back the 'old holidays with their mirth and rights', adding 'feasting daily will be in Merry England, for England is so plentiful of all provisions, that if we do not eat them, they will eat us, so we feast in our defence'.

For country recreations the duke recommended:

May games, morris dances, the Lords of the May, and Lady of the May, the fool – and the hobby horse must not be forgotten. Also the Whitsun Lord and Lady, thrashing of hens at shrove-tide, carols and wassails at Christmas with good plum porridge and pies which now are forbidden as profane ungodly things, wakes – fairs and markets maintain commerce and trade – and after evening prayer every Sunday and Holiday, the country people with their fresher lasses to trip on the town green about the May pole, to the louder bagpipe there to be refreshed with their ales and cakes …

Not only did he remind Charles about his grandfather's declaration on sports but he also suggested amusements that King James had disliked – tumblers and jugglers and plays. Just as people today believe that sports stop young people from hooliganism, so the duke claimed: 'The divertisements will amuse the people's thoughts, and keep them in harmless action which will free your Majesty from faction and rebellion.' He saw them as a way of promoting an alliance between the lower sort of people and the gentry and the monarchy.

When Charles II came back, many towns and country villages were of the duke's opinion and brought back their country celebrations. 'Now, as the morn grows lighter and lighter, and more glorious, till it is perfect day, so it was with the joy of the people,' wrote John Aubrey. 'Maypoles … now were set up in every cross way: and at the Strand, near Drury Lane, was set up the most prodigious one for height, that perhaps was ever seen.' The churchwardens at Campden paid out three shillings, a large sum, to bellringers to ring in the Restoration, and a further £3 10s 8d was spent on painting the royal arms in the church.

With the maypoles and the bells came a revival of Dover's Olimpicks. We do not know the exact date of their new beginning, nor whether Robert Dover's son John had a part in it, but start they did. Later on it was a grandson, Thomas Dover, a doctor best known for a popular remedy, Dover's Powders, who republished *Annalia Dubrensia*, probably around 1736, 'in memory of that good man his grandfather'.

But without the controlling influence of Robert Dover himself, the Games deteriorated. We have an account in the poem 'Hobbinol', written by William Somerville in 1740, which mentions wrestling and cudgel play and describes a general riot, suggesting that Dover's Games had become just another drunken country festival in which

> stools in pieces rent,
> And chairs, and forms, and battered bowls are hurled,
> With fell intent; like bombs the bottles fly

Hissing in air, their sharp-edged fragments drenched
In the warm spouting gore; heaps driven on heaps
Promiscuous lie.

As Somerville said in his introduction: 'A country wake is too sad an image of the infirmities of our own people. We see nothing but broken heads, bottles flying about, tables overturned, outrageous drunkenness, and eternal squabble.'

A description of the Games next surfaces in a novel, *The Spiritual Quixote*, written by the clergyman novelist Richard Graves and published in 1773. The novel's hero is a Methodist preacher, who disapproves of the 'great irregularities … practised amongst the common people upon those festivals, at wakes and revels and other ungodly meetings: particularly at a heathenish assembly of that kind, on the Cotswold hills, called Dover's meeting'.

It is significant that Richard Graves describes only 'two or three forlorn coaches' at the Games, not the large number of gentry who had attended in Dover's day. The coach parties had come, he writes, 'to contemplate the humours of these awkward rustics, and waste an hour of their tedious month in the country where (as a great modern observes)

small matters serve for amusement.' The gentry, who half a century before would have attended Dover's Olimpicks, had now deserted the Games.

One sport which marked the moral deterioration of the Games was a women's race with a smock for a prize – a saucy sport, which usually involved the girls hitching up their long skirts or even taking them off altogether in order to run more freely. 'Proclamation was made, that a holland shift, which was adorned with ribbands, and displayed on a pole, was going to be run for,' wrote Richard Graves, 'and six young women began to exhibit themselves before the whole assembly, in a dress hardly reconcilable to the rules of decency.'

By the eighteenth century, Dover's Olimpicks were beginning to look like a quaint survival from the past and were more likely to be thought of as Dover's Games than as Olimpick Games. But antiquarians began to notice them, as part of a new interest in folklore and folk festivals. In 1779 Samuel Rudder's *New History of Gloucestershire* described a typical Whitsun ale and wondered whether such festivals had 'their rise in Druidism'.

He went on to mention 'the Cotswold Games' and *Annalia Dubrensia*, quoted some of the poetry and remarked: 'Already we hear but little on the Cotswolds of his worthy friend, Mr Dover, since whose time the diversions have also much declined, for want of so good a patron.' He adds a Latin quote from Horace translated as: 'What doth not Time's injurious hand impair?'

Posters of the nineteenth century labelled the Games as 'Dover's Meetings'. There were still backsword contests, wrestling and women's dancing, but there was also a donkey race in 1806 with a prize of one guinea, cock fighting and bowling. A little later, jingling is added to the sports. This was a sort of blindman's buff except that all participants had a blindfold except the jingler. Wearing bells on his knees and elbows, the jingler's part was to be 'it', to avoid being caught despite the noise of his bells.

The Games were becoming more rural and less respect-able even if the 1819 poster claimed they 'have been the admiration of all honest, learned and well-disposed Britons for upwards of two centuries, and which are now patronised and esteemed by all noble, brave, and liberal minded men, who have a sincere and true regard for their native country'.

The backsword contests still required brave men. At the beginning of the nineteenth century, a particularly famous fight took place between Mr Ebenezer Prestage of Chipping Campden and a Mr Spyres of Mickleton. It went on so long that the combatants had to be separated, and Mr Spyres was so badly injured that he died soon after. The wrestling competitions had now become shin-kicking. Sometimes the combatants were shod with heavy nailed boots with metal tips. Occasionally the tips were pointed.

By 1845 the Dover Games were organised by a Chipping Campden publican, William Drury. He paid £5 for the right to do so, let out space to stalls and booths and presumably sold drink on the hill. The local rector of Weston sub Edge, the Revd Geoffrey Drinkwater Bourne, made the unlikely claim that up to 30,000 people were now attending the Games, and an even less likely claim that the hillside was full of drunk and disorderly people. It was said that nowadays no gentlemen attended the occasion. Just as the Puritans of the seventeenth century had blamed church ales for drunkenness and disorder, so the moral reformers of the Victorian era had no liking for the rougher country sports. Sometimes as puritanical as their predecessors of the seventeenth century, they suppressed low-life pastimes like cock fighting and dog fighting while allowing the high-life pastime of hunting and coursing to continue.

The Revd Bourne was the source for the remarks made by R. R. Vyvyan, who reprinted *Annalia Dubrensia* in 1878. Vyvyan wrote:

From 1846 onwards, the games, instead of being as they originally were intended to be decorously conducted, became the trysting place of all the lowest scum of the population which lived in the districts lying between Birmingham and Oxford. These people came to Dover's Hill and remained there the

whole of Whitsun week, creating all sorts of disturbances, and in short demoralizing the whole neighbourhood ... It is a great pity that Englishmen of
the 19th century were unable to conduct themselves
with the decorum and propriety of their ancestors of
150 years previously.

A generation later, the son of a woman who had kept a
booth on the hill claimed that 'no one was safe from the
lawlessness of the crowd of card-sharpers, thimble-riggers,
vagrants, pickpockets, thieves, confidence-men, vagrants and
criminals of the deepest dye, the riff-raff of society'.

This account was the official version for many years, but
it may have been exaggerated. The historian C. J. Bearman
has examined the diary of the police superintendent at
Chipping Campden. There are entries such as 'Proceeded
to Dovershill with a party of Constables to prevent a prize
fight that I had received information would take place.
Remained there from 6pm until 9pm, all being very quiet
and orderly withdrew the Constables ...' And in the local
magistrates' courts, there are no records of men being prosecuted for drunkenness or fighting.

One of the main factors in closing down the Games was economic. The land was still held in common by several people in an open-field system, and local landowners wanted to be able to fence off their share of it. Most of the common land in Gloucestershire had been parcelled off and fenced in the century before. The common land of Chipping Campden, for instance, had gone in 1819.

The existence of the Olimpicks depended on the retention of common land, pasture rather than cornfields. As far back as the original *Annalia Dubrensia*, one of the poets had presciently linked the Games with the common land. Shackerley Marmion had condemned the 'bad owners of enclosèd grounds'. And by the second half of the nineteenth century the common land above Weston sub Edge was an anachronistic survival. The Assistant Commissioners of 1850, giving consent for enclosure, declared: 'We consider this proposed inclosure expedient on the ground that the common land is divided by the baulks and cannot be profitably or conveniently cultivated in its present state.' So a total of 969 acres was distributed between local farmers and landowners. The Revd G. D. Bourne, who had complained of the disturbances at the Games, received 63 acres.

Shackerley Marmion's condemnation of men whose 'souls are narrow as their bounds' (i.e. their boundaries) had been proved prophetic. Once again the Puritans had succeeded in banning the Games. If there were individuals who cherished an Olympic ideal and wanted their Olimpicks saved, their voices were not heard. The Olimpick flame was snuffed out for the second time.

TO HIS WORTHY FRIEND
Mr Robert Dover,
ON HIS FAMOUS YEARLY
ASSEMBLIES UPON COTSWOLD

To write thy praises how shall I begin,
O noble Dover, who has brought us in
Pastimes of which, though we have often read,
Yet ne'er before did see them practisèd …

For when thy several pastimes shall be viewed,
Who will not think the Golden Age renewed?
The country lasses, in the midst of mirth,
Shall think of thee, that gave their pleasures birth;
Shepherds thy praise shall sing in well-tuned verse,
And even the rural swains thy fame rehearse.
Lords, Ladies, shepherds, country people all,
Shall speak in praise of Dover's festival.
  And when thou'rt dead, all sorts of men shall strive,
  Although not thee, to keep thy fame alive.

JOHN MONSON

Chapter 7

RECLAIMING OUR
Olimpick Heritage

The birth of a new Olympic ideal, that was eventually to lead to the modern Olympic Games, took place just at the time that the Revd G. D. Bourne collected his 63 acres and played his part in closing down Dover's Olimpicks. It is an irony of history that, if Dover's Games had managed to continue for another ten years, they might have become an important festival for those who were interested in a revival of the original Olympics.

For the idea of reviving the Olympics as modern games had its genesis in the nineteenth century. As early as 1835, while Dover's Games were still flourishing, a Greek poet,

Panagiotis Soutsos, put forward a proposal to do so in his native country. And though the first modern Greek Olympic Games would not occur for another twenty-six years, Soutsos continued year by year to campaign for their revival.

Meanwhile the first stirrings of the modern Olympic movement in Britain (other than Robert Dover's) came from a Victorian doctor. William Penny Brookes, of Much Wenlock, Shropshire, was as anxious to improve the lot of working men as Canon Bourne had been to curb their enjoyments. First he formed a reading society to improve their minds, and then he decided to help their bodies too.

In 1850 he formed the Wenlock Olympian Class, holding the first games that year and annually from then on. The Wenlock Games, like the Dover Games before them, were not a slavish imitation of the ancient ones and were mainly a local affair, though some events were open to outsiders. His purpose was to 'promote the moral, physical and intellectual improvement of the inhabitants of the town and neighbourhood of Wenlock'.

At various they

included a cricket match, a football match, quoits, and hopping on one leg, as well as the more Olympian high jump, long jump and foot races.

In some ways Brookes looked backwards rather than forwards. With a Victorian love of the medieval, he introduced 'tilting at the ring', a sport that was dying out even in Robert Dover's day. There is a charming picture of the first herald of the games in 1867 – Thomas Yates, a boy dressed up in the Victorian idea of medieval costume. Brookes also ran mathematics and knitting contests and, recalling the odes of the ancient Greek poet Pindar, gave a prize for the best poem on the Games.

Did William Penny Brookes know about Robert Dover? In starting his own Wenlock Games, the doctor was influenced by Joseph Strutt's book, *Sports and Pastimes of the People of England*. He borrowed from this for his choice of sports at the Wenlock Games, and in it he would have read of Robert Dover's Games in a section titled 'Cotswold and Cornish Games'. 'I should mention the annual celebration of games upon Cotswold Hills, in Gloucestershire,' wrote Strutt, 'to which prodigious multitudes constantly resorted. Robert Dover, an attorney, of Barton on the Heath, in the country of Warwick was forty years the chief direct of these pastimes.'

But there was a crucial omission in this passage to Dover's Games – no mention of Olimpick Games. Instead, the passage passes from the Cotswold Games to games held on Bodmin Moor in Cornwall, which were 'said to be as old as the Saxons'. When William Penny Brookes read this passage the supposedly Saxon origin of the Cornish Games would probably have caught his eye, and he would have had no reason to associate the Cotswold Games with ancient Greece.

Later Brookes might have read Chambers' *Book of Days*, published in 1862, where he would have noticed a mention of the Games. Antiquarians were taking an interest in *Annalia Dubrensia* by now, and two editions of the book were published, in 1877 and 1878. But there is no record of William Penny Brookes knowing about them or taking any particular interest in the former existence of Robert Dover's Olimpicks.

Perhaps if he had known more about Dover's Games, he might have done something to revive them or, instead of tilting at a quintain, chosen to follow Dover's choice of sports more closely. Brookes was a man with a sense of what might be done to revive a historical event. He made contact with the Greek campaigners for modern Olympic Games and later was in touch with the great Pierre de Coubertin, and can fairly be described as one of the forefathers of the modern Olympic movement.

Baron Coubertin visited Wenlock in 1890 and games were arranged in his honour by the now elderly doctor. Coubertin even called Dr Brookes 'my oldest friend'. Alas, Brookes died a few months before the first international Olympic Games in 1896.

While the Wenlock Games were flourishing, the original Kingcombe Plain was fenced, enclosed and split between various farmers, rich landowners and, of course, the vicar. Much of what had been pasture was ploughed up and the race course, which had been several miles long, also fell to the plough. Only one section of the hill, with an enormously steep slope, remained as pasture and woodland. It was this part of the hill which kept the name of Robert Dover alive.

Even this came under threat. In 1929 the land was put up for sale as a possible site for a new hotel, a development

that in those days would have required no form of plan-
ning permission. It was a local artist, Frederick Landseer
Griggs, who saved the site. Though he could ill afford to
do so, he bid against the developers at auction and bought
the land for £4,000. Had he not ventured his own money
in this way any rescue attempt would have been too late.
Over the next two years an appeal was launched and,
with financial help from the historian T. M. Trevelyan,
Dover's Hill was bought back from Griggs and given to
the National Trust. Today it is grazing land and woodland
with a circular walk.

Once the natural amphitheatre of Dover's Hill's steep
escarpment was safe, the revival of Dover's Games became
a possibility. Though the Dover Games had ceased, a local
celebration called the Scuttlebrook Wake had persisted.
It was held on the Saturday after Whitsun in Chipping
Campden and was a traditional local event including dancing and a torchlight procession.

It was in 1951 that Dover's Games were revived in
modern times. This was the year of the Festival of Britain
and local people put on a week of celebrations, starting
with a procession on Whit Monday in nearby Chipping

Campden and ending with the Scuttlebrook Wake the following Saturday.

The revived Robert Dover's Cotswold Olimpicks were held on the hill. In the tradition of the original Games there were 'equestrian sports', boxing, a tug of war, donkey races and foot races. From the folk flavour of the nineteenth-century Games came modern equivalents – pillow fights, climbing the greasy pole, horseshoe throwing, coconut shies and bowling for a pig. The most popular survival was probably the shin-kicking.

It was at this 1951 revival that Robert Dover, in the shape of a local rider dressed in historical costume, rode again for the first time – the outward and visible sign that the man is not forgotten. By so doing, the revived Games paid a graceful tribute to the seventeenth-century jovial lawyer. And in today's Games he still rides among the onlookers – nowadays in the company of Endymion Porter. Both are mounted and dressed in the Cavalier clothes of their time.

Originally it was hoped that the 1951 Dover Olimpicks would be a yearly fixture. But an outbreak of foot-and-mouth in the locality meant they could not be held the following year, and 1953 saw the coronation of Queen Elizabeth II, celebrated in almost every town and village of the country, so once again the Games were not held.

It was in 1952 that Robert Dover's Olimpicks caught the attention of Dr Francis Burns, a man who might be called its official historian. During his time at Oxford University Burns had been intrigued to discover the existence of the seventeenth-century Games and a few years later began to write an MA thesis upon their history, finally completing this in 1960. Two years later another historian, Christopher Whitfield, author of a local history of Chipping Campden, republished *Annalia Dubrensia* with an account of the Games.

The next revival of the Games on Dover's Hill came as part of the 1964 Scuttlebrook Wake when, on the Friday before the Saturday Wake, a torchlight procession started at Dover's Hill and continued down to Chipping Campden Square. In the procession was a mounted Robert Dover again. This was repeated the following year, and since then the Olimpicks have been established on the Friday evening of Whitsun week.

It was a few weeks after the Wake of 1965 that the Robert Dover's Games Society was formed out of the Scuttlebrook fête committee, to raise money in advance and to organise 'the revival of Robert Dover's Cotswold Games according to present day tastes'. Now it has its own website – www.olimpickgames.co.uk.

From then onwards the Games took on new life. In 1966 a pack of hounds came to the event, there were gymkhana events, motor cycle displays, a tug of war, a greasy pole and that old Cotswold favourite, shin-kicking. The evening ended with a bonfire and a torchlight procession to Chipping Campden Square.

This pattern has continued ever since. Each year there are variations on the theme. The Games have, in various years, included dwile flonking (an invented folkloric sport involving wet floorcloths), climbing for the popinjay, motor cycle scrambling, judo, piano smashing, sack racing in huge sacks, parachute jumping, balloon ascents, morris dancing not forgetting the hobby horse, and even (in 1976) a poetry competition.

Some years have had an exhibition of backswording or cudgel play but without broken heads and slashed flesh. Shin-kicking is still an annual favourite. This too is a much gentler event than the original. Competitors are allowed to protect their shins with padding and shoes are no longer tipped with iron.

The Robert Dover's Games Society even researched the possibility of recreating Dover's castle in its original form. Historian Matthew Alexander created a scale model based on the original illustration. 'I did a lot of research and based the structure on the rotating windmills of the time. The problem wasn't making it strong enough nor was the problem the expense.'

The difficulty facing the Society was that the dismantled rotating castle would have included some very large pieces of wood, which would have been difficult to store. It would also have required expertise to reassemble and erect it each year. In fact, the Society already had a simpler mock castle, so they opted to retain their existing castle, without a pivotal base. The modern castle can be seen on the hillside today at the Games.

Dr Francis Burns, whose MA had been the first piece of careful research of the twentieth century, had now moved back into the area and wrote an official book of the Games, *Heigh for Cotswold! Robert Dover's Olimpick Games*. It was also around this time that the Dover's Olimpicks became recognised for what they were – the first ever English Games on an Olympic model. A special booklet was produced at the time of Birmingham's bid for the Olympic Games – *Britain and the Olympic Games, Rediscovery of a Heritage* by Don Anthony, a former Olympian hammer thrower. At last Robert Dover could take his place in Olympic history.

Yet the Olimpicks on Dover's Hill have stayed relatively simple and determinedly local. They are not a mere re-enactment of the kind seen among societies like the Sealed Knot, where people from all over the country come to dress up in period clothes to re-enact history. They are run by local people for local people and include competitions and events that appeal to the regulars.

'We are an organisation where the committee is made up of all comers, people with different talents of all kinds,' says Dr Francis Burns. Nor is alcohol sold on the hill during the celebrations. There are no beer tents and thus no fear of drunkenness of the kind that so shocked the Victorian vicar. In this it is close to the original Games, policed by Robert Dover to make sure there was no disorder. TV cameras and outside onlookers are now common, but there are no plans to upgrade the event into a national one.

The major problems that face the continuing Games are those that face any rural outdoor festival – an agricultural animal epidemic and bad weather. A downpour in 1977 left only £5 in the bank balance and the Games were shut down altogether in the year 2001, when a foot-and-mouth epidemic raged in Britain. Such years test the Society's bank balance to its utmost.

In order to ensure the Games' survival, the Society, while

giving support to local charities, has been careful to build up a bank balance that will survive a bad year. So the future looks safe for the survival of Robert Dover's Cotswold Games, as long as people assemble on the hill to watch or participate in harmless sports.

The fame of Robert Dover and his first ever English Olimpicks is still alive.

References

Anthony, Don, *Britain and the Olympic Games, Rediscovery of a Heritage,* 1986.

Anthony, Don, *Minds, Bodies and Souls,* 3 vols, 1995.

Aubrey, John, *Natural History of Wiltshire,* ed. John Britton, 1847.

Aubrey, John, *Miscellanies upon Various Subjects,* 1857.

Aubrey, John, *Brief Lives,* with a Life of John Aubrey, ed. Andrew Clark, 1898.

Aubrey, John, *Remains of Gentilisme and Judaisme, Three Prose Works,* 1972.

Barksdale, Clement, *Nympha Libethris or The Cotswold Muse,* 1651.

Barnard, E, *Evesham and Four Shires, Notes & Queries,* 1911.

Brand, John, *Observations on the Popular Antiquities of Great Britain,* 1849.

Brown, Terry, *English Martial Arts,* Anglo-Saxon Books, 1997.

Burns, Francis, 'Robert Dover's Cotswold Olimpick Games; the use of the term "Olimpick"', *Olympic Review,* no. 210, April 1985, pp. 231–6.

Burns, Francis, *Heigh for Cotswold! Robert Dover's Olimpick Games*, 2000.

Burns, Francis, *Robert Dover's Cotswold Olimpicks. The Twentieth Century Games from the Festival of Britain to the Millennium*, 2000.

Burton, Henry, *A Divine Tragedie Lately Enacted*, 1636.

Burton, Robert, *The Anatomy of Melancholy*, 1621.

Cleland, James, *The Institution of a Young Noble Man*, 1607.

Cotton, Charles, *The Compleat Gamester*, 1674.

Croome, W. I., 'Lodge Park, Aldsworth, Glos. and Rules for Coursing', *Transactions of the Bristol and Gloucestershire Archaeology Society*, vol. 82, 1963, pp. 212–14.

Douthwaite, William Ralph, *Gray's Inn. Its History and Associations*, 1886.

Earle, John, *Microcosmographie*, 1628.

Elyot, Sir Thomas, *The Book named The Governor*, 1531.

Hill, Christopher, *Olympic Politics, Athens to Atlanta 1896–1996*, 1996.

Hoby, Thomas, *The Courtier*, 1561.

Hope, Sir William, *The Compleat Fencing Master*, 1691.

Hunt, E. M., *New Hampshire Town Names and Whence They Came*, 1970.

Hutton, Ronald, *The Rise and Fall of Merry England*, 1994.

Huxley, Gervas, *Endymion Porter*, 1959.

Jewell, Brian, *Sports and Games. History and Origins*, 1977.

References

King James VI and I, *Political Writings*, including *Basilicon Doron* and speeches to Parliament, ed. Johann P. Sommerville, 1994.

Lovesey, Peter, *The Official Centenary History of the Amateur Athletic Association*, 1979.

Madden, D. H., *Diary of Master Silence*, 1907.

Markham, Gervase, *Cheap and Good Husbandry*, 1657.

Mulcaster, Richard, *Positions*, 1581.

Mullins, Sam, *British Olympians. William Penny Brookes and the Wenlock Games*, 1992.

Northbrooke, John, *A Treatise wherein Dicing, Dauncing, Vain plays or Interludes with other idle pastimes …*, 1579.

Parkyns, Sir Thomas, *The Inn Play or Cornish Hugg Wrestler*, 1714.

Parmiter, Geoffrey, *Elizabethan Popish Recusancy in the Inns of Court*, 1976.

Peacham, Henry, *The Compleat Gentleman*, 1622.

Powell, Geoffrey, *The Book of Camden*, 1982.

Reeve, Edmund, *The Communion Book Catechism Expounded*, 1636.

Rudder, Samuel, *A New History of Gloucestershire*, 1779.

Sidney, Sir Philip, *An Apology for Poetry*, 1595.

Somerville, William, *The Poetical Works*, 1805.

Stallybrass, Peter, ' "Wee feaste in our Defense": Patrician Carnival in Early Modern England and Robert Herrick's "Hesperides"', *English Literary Renaissance*, vol. 16, no. 1, Winter 1986, pp. 234–52.

Stallybrass, Peter, 'Worn Worlds: Clothes and Identity on the Renaissance Stage', in *Subject and Object in Renaissance Culture*, ed. M. De Grazia *et al.*, 1996.

Stewart, Alan, *The Cradle King. A Life of James VI and I*, 2003.

Strong, S. Arthur, *A Catalogue of Letters and Other Historical Documents Exhibited in the Library at Welbeck*, 1903.

Strutt, Joseph, *Sports and Pastimes of the People of England*, 1810.

Stubbes, Philip, *The Anatomie of Abuses*, 1583.

Swaddling, Judith, *The Ancient Olympic Games*, 1999.

Tomalin, Claire, *Samuel Pepys, The Unequalled Self*, 2002.

Townsend, Dorothea, *The Life and Letters of Mr Endymion Porter*, 1897.

Trollope, E., 'Notices of Ancient and Medieval Labyrinths', *Archaeological Journal*, XV, pp. 216–35, 1858.

Vale, Marcia, *The Gentleman's Recreation*, 1977.

Waugh, Norah, *The Cut of Men's Clothes 1600–1900*, 1964.

Whitfield, Christopher, *A History of Chipping Campden and Captain Robert Dover's Olympic Games*, 1958.

Whitfield, Christopher, *Robert Dover and the Cotswold Games, A New Edition of* Annalia Dubrensia, 1962.

Wood, Anthony à, *Athenae Oxoniensis*, vol. 4, ed. with additions by Philip Bliss, 1820.

Young, David C., *The Modern Olympics. A Struggle for Revival*, 1996.